An Old French Trilogy

UNIVERSITY PRESS OF FLORIDA

Florida A&M University, Tallahassee
Florida Atlantic University, Boca Raton
Florida Gulf Coast University, Ft. Myers
Florida International University, Miami
Florida State University, Tallahassee
New College of Florida, Sarasota
University of Central Florida, Orlando
University of Florida, Gainesville
University of North Florida, Jacksonville
University of South Florida, Tampa
University of West Florida, Pensacola

An Old French Trilogy

Texts from the William of Orange Cycle

TRANSLATED BY

Catherine M. Jones,

William W. Kibler,

and Logan E. Whalen

UNIVERSITY PRESS OF FLORIDA

Gainesville / Tallahassee / Tampa / Boca Raton

Pensacola / Orlando / Miami / Jacksonville / Ft. Myers / Sarasota

25 24 23 22 21 20   6 5 4 3 2 1

Library of Congress Cataloging-in-Publication Data
Names: Jones, Catherine M. (Catherine Mary), 1956– translator, editor. |
Kibler, William W., 1942– translator, editor. | Whalen, Logan E., translator, editor.
Title: An old French trilogy : texts from the William of Orange cycle /
edited and translated by Catherine M. Jones, William W. Kibler, and Logan E. Whalen.
Description: Gainesville : University Press of Florida, 2020. | Includes
bibliographical references and index.
Identifiers: LCCN 2020001890 (print) | LCCN 2020001891 (ebook) | ISBN
9780813066462 (hardback) | ISBN 9780813057521 (pdf)
Subjects: LCSH: Guillaume d'Orange (Chansons de geste) | Epic poetry,
French—History and criticism. | Cycles (Literature)
Classification: LCC PQ1481.A3 J63 2020 (print) | LCC PQ1481.A3 (ebook) |
DDC 841/.0320801—dc23
LC record available at https://lccn.loc.gov/2020001890
LC ebook record available at https://lccn.loc.gov/2020001891

The University Press of Florida is the scholarly publishing agency for the State University
System of Florida, comprising Florida A&M University, Florida Atlantic University,
Florida Gulf Coast University, Florida International University, Florida State University,
New College of Florida, University of Central Florida, University of Florida, University
of North Florida, University of South Florida, and University of West Florida.

University Press of Florida
2046 NE Waldo Road
Suite 2100
Gainesville, FL 32609
http://upress.ufl.edu

Contents

Acknowledgments

We are grateful to a number of people who aided in the completion of this book. We deeply appreciate the time and effort of Dahlia J. Riley, Laura Scott, and Sandra Whalen, who read our manuscript and made helpful recommendations. Laura Scott in particular spent countless hours meticulously reading our work at various stages. Her sharp editorial skills caught errors we would have overlooked, and her numerous suggestions allowed us to present a clean final manuscript to the press. We offer our thanks to Sandra Whalen for her close reading of the proofs.

We also wish to recognize the aesthetic and intellectual contributions of several friends and colleagues. Monica Wright's expertise in medieval textiles and clothing guided us in rendering into modern English the names of numerous garments particular to the period of our texts. Abigail Grace Kelly gave visual form to the local geography of the time of William of Orange's fictional deeds through her carefully constructed map. We owe the book's cover to Debra L. Bell, who provided the beautiful photograph of the Abbey of Gellone in Saint-Guilhem-le-Désert.

At the University Press of Florida we are grateful for the generous assistance of Rachel Welton, Marthe Walters, and especially Stephanye Hunter, who believed in our work from the very beginning and ensured that it came to fruition. We acknowledge and heartily thank the anonymous outside readers of our manuscript. Their close reading and thoughtful comments significantly improved our work. It also benefited substantially from the professional eyes of the copy editor, Ann Marlowe.

Finally, we dedicate this book to our spouses, Richard Neupert, Nancy Kibler, and Sandra Whalen. Simply put, this book would not exist without their unwavering support and encouragement.

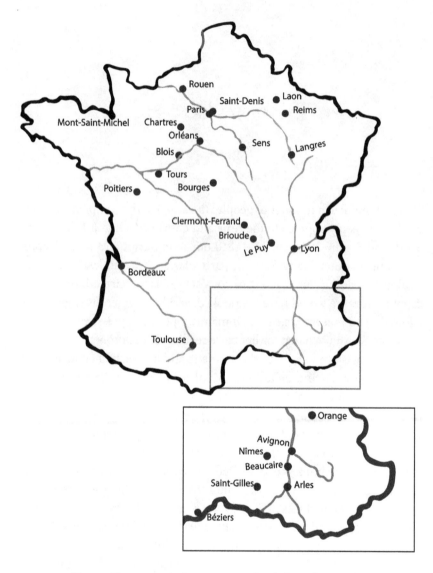

Figure 1. Place-names in France associated with the William Cycle.
Map created by Abigail Grace Kelly.

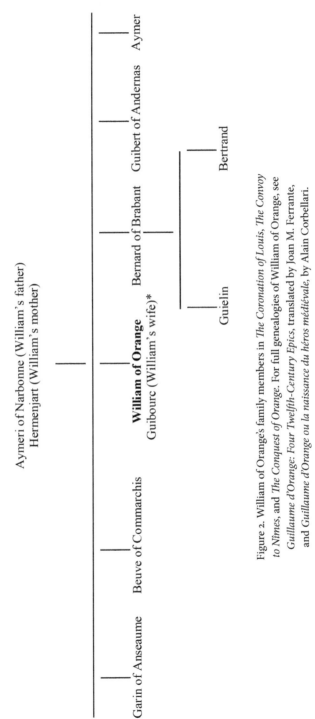

Figure 2. William of Orange's family members in *The Coronation of Louis*, *The Convoy to Nîmes*, and *The Conquest of Orange*. For full genealogies of William of Orange, see *Guillaume d'Orange: Four Twelfth-Century Epics*, translated by Joan M. Ferrante, and *Guillaume d'Orange ou la naissance du héros médiévale*, by Alain Corbellari.

Aymeri of Narbonne (William's father)
Hermenjart (William's mother)

Garin of Anseaume   Beuve of Commarchis   **William of Orange**   Bernard of Brabant   Guibert of Andernas   Aymer
                                            Guibourc (William's wife)*

Guielin   Bertrand

Introduction

The Chansons de Geste

The three poems presented in this volume belong to the large and varied corpus of Old French epics, or chansons de geste.[1] Among the earliest and most enduring forms of vernacular poetic production in medieval France, the chansons de geste are so designated because of their shared roots in an orally transmitted heroic tradition. They are called *chansons,* songs, by virtue of their musical dimension. Though the manuscripts do not contain musical notation, evidence from textual and iconographical sources suggests that the earliest extant works (and/or their lost antecedents) were sung by professional entertainers called jongleurs. Melodies were undoubtedly limited to a simple chant, and were often accompanied by a vielle, a type of medieval fiddle. Composed of *laisses,* or stanzas of varying length, the chansons de geste exhibit a lyrical structure that persisted throughout the medieval period, even when the "songs" came to be recited or read aloud. The word *geste* refers to the subject matter associated with the epic. A feminine noun in Old French, *geste* derives from the Latin plural *gesta* and designates great deeds or feats of arms. *Geste* can also refer to a family or lineage, a chronicle or account, and, by extension, a group of epic songs about a particular lineage. The chanson de geste may thus be broadly defined as "a song or stanzaic poem celebrating the exploits of a hero or clan."[2] The corpus contains approximately 120 works dating from the late eleventh to the early fifteenth century.

Although most chansons de geste are set in the distant past, in the eighth and ninth centuries, they tend to portray the sociopolitical structures and values that were prevalent during their time of composition.

The works presented in this volume were all composed in the twelfth century, during the age of feudalism. Like other epics of the period, these poems depict a society that depended on a complex set of mutual obligations binding overlords to their vassals. An overlord was obligated to protect his vassal and, increasingly, was expected to grant him a fief that eventually became a hereditary possession. A vassal was bound to provide counsel and military service, as well as unwavering loyalty. The chansons de geste explore the tensions and fissures in the feudal system, including the growing rivalry between monarchs and powerful feudal lords, territorial and matrimonial disputes, and insufficiencies in judicial custom. In addition, the Crusades (1095–1291) inform the plots of the numerous epic narratives centered around Christian-Muslim conflict. In keeping with the crusading ethos, which called upon the European warrior aristocracy to defend Christianity against the military and cultural forces of Islam, many French epic heroes set out to reconquer Muslim-controlled cities or reclaim disputed holy sites. Serving partly as instruments of religious and social propaganda, the epics demonize the Muslim Other and embrace a poetics of violence. These poems were also a form of popular historiography, often taking historical figures or battles as a point of departure and distorting them to suit their narrative or political purposes.[3] Mediated by the emphatic voice of a narrator-jongleur, the chansons de geste invite participation in a collective, commemorative experience.

The William of Orange Cycle

Most of the Old French epics are attached to "cycles" (also known as *gestes*), groups of chansons de geste clustered around a particular hero, lineage, or thematic connection.[4] The Old French epic tradition is known to modern English-speaking audiences almost exclusively through *La Chanson de Roland* (*The Song of Roland*), the foundational text of the Charlemagne cycle. This work is justly appreciated for its masterful depiction of betrayal, heroic martyrdom, and retribution. The *Roland* is not, however, representative of the genre as a whole. In an effort to provide a broader and richer view of the tradition, the present volume is devoted to the exploits of a very different sort of hero, the brave and blustery Guillaume d'Orange (William of Orange).[5] Like many Old French epic heroes, William of Orange is loosely based on a historical figure, William, Count of Toulouse (ca. 755–812).[6] A cousin of Charlemagne, William of Toulouse was defeated by Muslim forces at the Battle of Orbieu in 793 but captured Barcelona in 803. Toward the end of his life, he retired to the monastery of Aniane and founded the Abbey of Gellone, which was later renamed Saint-Guilhem-le-Désert. The epic and historical figures follow similar trajectories (as will be evident below) and were already assimilated by the early twelfth century, before the appearance of the extant poems. The epic William's (fictional) conquest of Orange, for example, appears in the 1125 *Vita sancti Wilhelmi* (Life of St. William) to embellish the career of William of Toulouse. It is clear that a legendary William narrative was circulating even earlier. A Latin summary of the Roland legend known as the *Nota Emilianense* (ca. 1065–1075) mentions among Charlemagne's peers a "Ghigelmo alcorbitanas" (crooked-nosed William), one version of the epic William's most prominent physical trait.[7]

The cycle that formed around this figure, known variously as the "cycle of William of Orange" or the "cycle of Garin of Monglane,"[8] comprises twenty-four epic poems devoted to William and his extended family. Most of these poems have come down to us in "cyclical manuscripts" that gather and organize individual songs according to fictional chronology. Literary historians distinguish two foundational clusters at the heart of the William cycle.[9] The three poems presented here, *Le Couronnement de Louis* (*The Coronation of Louis,* ca. 1150), *Le Charroi de Nîmes* (*The Convoy to Nîmes,* ca. 1150), and *La Prise d'Orange* (*The Conquest of Orange,* ca. 1160), form the core of William's early heroic biography. In *The Coronation of Louis,* the hero saves both king and pope from would-be usurpers and earns the nickname "short-nosed William" after a fierce, disfiguring battle with a Saracen giant. In *The Convoy to Nîmes* and *The Conquest of Orange,* William conquers two important cities and wins the love of the Saracen queen Orable. The popularity of the triad in the Middle Ages is attested by the manuscript tradition: the texts are preserved sequentially in eight cyclical manuscripts, where they form a virtually continuous narrative of William's (fictional) early victories against enemies of the church and the crown.[10]

A second cluster was generated by *La Chanson de Guillaume* (*The Song of William,* ca. 1150), which survives in a single noncyclical manuscript. Though it contains some of the earliest material devoted to William, this work depicts the mature hero and his later struggles against redoubtable Saracen forces. At the battle of l'Archamp, William suffers a series of setbacks, including the loss of his beloved nephew Vivien, whose poignant death scene has often been compared to Roland's last stand. William manages to defeat the enemy only with the help of his wife Guibourc (formerly Orable) and a rough-edged giant named Rainouart, who is revealed to be Guibourc's long-lost brother. In the cyclical manuscripts, the events recounted in the *Song of William* are reworked and incorporated into the late twelfth-century *Aliscans*. The final installment of William's biography appears in *Le Moniage Guillaume* (*William's Monastic Life*, late twelfth century), in which the hero, widowed and repentant, renounces warfare in favor of a monastic life to which he is comically ill-suited. After emerging from retirement to accomplish a few spectacular final deeds, William ends his days as a hermit in the place now known as Saint-Guilhem-le-Désert.

The William cycle expanded in the later twelfth and thirteenth centuries to include poems devoted to William's ancestors, nephews, brothers, and brother-in-law Rainouart. An anonymous fifteenth-century prose version of the cycle, *Le Roman de Guillaume d'Orange* (*The Romance of William of Orange*), demonstrates the enduring appeal of the William material throughout the French Middle Ages. Adaptations in other languages attest to the cycle's diffusion among a larger European audience. A Middle High German poem, Wolfram von Eschenbach's unfinished *Willehalm* (1210–1220), incorporates elements of *The Conquest of Orange*. Fragments in Middle Dutch point to the existence of multiple versions in the Low Countries. In Italy, the fifteenth-century Florentine author Andrea da Barberino rendered a substantial portion of the cycle into his prose *Storie Nerbonese* (*Stories of Narbonne*).[11]

Form and Style

The chansons de geste exhibit a distinctive formal composition derived from their origins in oral-formulaic poetry. Most of the early works, including the three poems in this volume, were composed in assonanced, decasyllabic laisses.[12] Patterns of repetition highlight not only important moments in the narrative but also the contours of the epic stanza.[13] For example, the device known as *enchaînement,* or linking, creates a bridge between two laisses by recounting the same action at the end of one laisse and the beginning of the next. In the following passage from *The Conquest of Orange,* the Saracens' imprisonment of William and his companions at the end of laisse 53 is immediately recalled at the threshold of laisse 54:

Guillelme font en la chartre gitier	They had William thrown into the cell,
Et Guïelin, qui preuz fu et legier,	And brave and agile Guielin,
Et dame Orable avec els trebuchier.	And Lady Orable was tossed in with them.
Or en penst Deu qui tot a a jugier!	May God who judges all watch over them!

54.

Or fu Guillelmes trebuchiez en la chartre	Now William was thrown into the cell
Et Guïelin et la cortoise Orable;	Along with Guielin and courtly Orable;
Sovent se claime maleüreuse lasse:	She often regretted her unhappy state:

(lines 1539–45)[14]

Repetition is enhanced by variation. The change in assonance (from *ie* to feminine *a*) marks the shift to a new laisse, and similar content is expressed with slight modifications of vocabulary and syntax. As is often the case with this type of repetition, each iteration of the protagonists' imprisonment presents the action from a slightly different perspective or grammatical aspect. Having first narrated the process in laisse 53 (Saracen rulers having the victims tossed into a cell), the narrator subsequently considers the scene as a completed action generating reactions or consequences. According to Jean Rychner, this device reconciles narrative and lyrical exigencies, marshaling the poem's musical structure in the service of narrative transitions.[15]

Strophic repetition of another sort groups two or more stanzas depicting the same basic action performed successively by different characters, or a series of objects or characters described in parallel form. An example of such "parallel" laisses may be found in *The Convoy to Nîmes* at the outset of William's expedition to reclaim Nîmes from the Saracens, when the narrator in laisses 26–28 describes the equipment loaded onto packhorses:

Bien vos sai dire que porte li premiers:	I can tell you what the first one carried:
Calices d'or et messeaus et sautiers,	Golden chalices and missals and psalters,

Chapes de paile et croiz et encensiers;	Silken copes and crosses and censers;
Quant il venront enz el regne essillié,	When they arrive in the devastated realm,
Serviront tuit Damedieu tot premier.	They will all first serve the Lord.

27.

Bien vos sai dire que reporte li autres:	I can tell you what the second one carried:
Vesseaus d'or fin, messeus et breviaire,	Vessels of pure gold, missals, and breviaries,
Et crucefis et molt riches toailles;	And crucifixes and precious altar cloths;
Quant il venront enz el regne sauvage,	When they come into the savage realm,
S'en serviront Jhesu l'esperitable.	They will be able to serve Jesus, the heavenly one.

28.

Bien vos sai dire que reporte li tierz:	I can tell you what the third one carried:
Poz et paielles, chauderons et trepiez,	Pots and pans, cauldrons and trivets,
Et croz aguz, tenailles et andiers;	And sharp hooks, tongs, and andirons;
Quant il venront enz el regne essillié,	Thus when they come to the devastated realm,
Que bien en puissent atorner a mengier.	They will be able to prepare food.

(lines 765–79)[16]

Parallel introductions and conclusions frame the three descriptions, highlighting the continuity between laisses 26 and 27 as well as the abrupt shift from religious objects to kitchen utensils in laisse 28. Underscored by the structural coherence of the three laisses, the humorous juxtaposition of spiritual and culinary concerns is all the more striking.

The most radical form of strophic repetition involves the reiteration of the same basic action—performed by the same character(s)—in two or more successive laisses or parts of laisses.[17] In these "similar" laisses, story time pauses, allowing the narrator-jongleur to dwell on a key moment. Attention shifts to lyric technique, as the same event is intoned with a different assonance, displaying slight variations in syntax and word choice. In *The Conquest of Orange,* for example, the device is used to highlight the Saracen king Aragon's dilemma when William and his two companions have succeeded in occupying the tower of Gloriette:

36.

"Faraon, sire, dist li rois Arragon,   "Pharaoh, sire," said King Aragon,

Car me donez bon conseil, por Mahom.   "Please give me good advice, by Mohammed.

Vez Glorïete, le palés et la tor,   Look there at Gloriette, the palace and tower:

Le fondement en est fet trusqu'en son;   It is built of stones all the way to the top;

Trestuit li home deci a Moncontor   All the men from here to Moncontour

Pas n'i feroient un pertuis contremont.   Couldn't make a crack from bottom to top.

Ou, vis deables, se prendroit le charbon?   Where, by the living devil, could you start the fire?

Il n'i a broche de fust ne de baston.   There's not a peg or stave of wood.

Par lor orgueill i sont cil troi gloton,   Those three scoundrels got in there by their audacity,

Devant .VII. anz n'en istront il par nos."   And we'll not get them out in seven years."

37.

"Faraon, sire, dit Arragon li rois,   "Pharaoh, sire," said King Aragon,

Por Mahomet, de qui tenons noz lois,   "By Mohammed, the source of our religion,

Car me donez bon conseil orendroit.   Give me some good advice right now!

Vez Glorïete, le palés majorois,   Look there at Gloriette, the main palace:

Li fondemenz en est fez a rochois;   Its foundations are made of stone;

Trestuit li home trusqu'as porz de Vanquois   All the men from here to the pass of Vauquois

Si n'i feroient un pertuis en un mois.	Couldn't crack them in a month.
A quex deables li charbons se prendroit,	How the devil can you start a fire
Quant n'i a broche de fust ne de lorois?	When there isn't a peg of wood or laurel?
Par lor orgueill i sont entré cil troi,	Those three scoundrels got in there by their audacity,
Devant .VII. ans n'en istront il par moi."	And I'll not get them out in seven years!"

(lines 1119–39)

Aragon's repeated lament emphasizes the tower's impregnability and sets the stage for the revelation of a hidden subterranean passageway that will allow the Saracens to penetrate Gloriette and imprison the Christian infiltrators.

Although they have come down to us as written documents, the chansons de geste, like other epic traditions, employ the structural tools associated with oral-formulaic composition.[18] Their subject matter favors the return of certain macro-narrative units, such as battles, council scenes, trials, and voyages. These larger themes are broken down into recurring motifs, highly conventional and stylized micro-narrative units that belong to the genre's storytelling repertory. Battle sequences, for example, are frequently depicted as a series of single combats, recounted in much the same way within a given poem and across the genre. The single-lance-combat motif is among the most codified. In its most developed form, the motif follows a time-honored sequence: the knight spurs his horse, brandishes his lance, strikes his adversary, pierces the adversary's shield, ruptures his hauberk, slays him (often slicing through his horse as well), and utters a cry of victory. Each component of the motif is rendered by one or more formulas, fixed phrases occurring regularly in the same metrical conditions to express a given idea.[19] Since the Old French epic decasyllabic line is typically divided into hemistichs of four and six syllables—a division known as epic caesura—formulas are fashioned within these constraints. In *The Coronation of Louis*, for example, the poet uses several variations of a six-syllable formula describing the knight's spurs: "des esperons agu(z)" (lines 1206, 1225, with his sharp spurs); "des esperons d'or mier" (line 2121, with his pure gold spurs); "des esperons forbiz" (line 2521, with his polished spurs). Other epic motifs, such as the premonitory dream, the epic credo uttered by a hero in extreme danger, the lament over a dead warrior, or the conversion of a Saracen princess, are less codified and more flexible in structure. It is important to emphasize that formulaic style was not a facile, automatized form of composition. Medieval audiences recognized and appreciated both the familiar strains of highly stereotyped motifs and the subtle variations that distinguished each usage. Like strophic repetition, conventional motifs and formulas contribute to the epic's incantatory quality.

The Texts

THE CORONATION OF LOUIS

The narrative falls into five distinct parts that may have originally existed as separate poems.[20]

After a conventional epic prologue promising a worthy song and a valiant story, the narrator recounts the coronation of Louis, son of Charlemagne. Considerably advanced in years, Charlemagne has decided to bestow the crown upon the fifteen-year-old Louis in order to ensure proper succession. Louis's reaction is characteristic of the weakness he will exhibit throughout the cycle: when summoned to accept the crown in the Royal Chapel, he freezes, prompting concern among the barons and outrage in his father. When the crafty Hernaut of Orléans attempts to usurp the throne, the mighty Count William strikes him dead and places the crown on young Louis's head (lines 1–149).

Shortly thereafter, William sets off on a pilgrimage to Rome, where he is soon called upon by the pope to repel a Saracen attack. The Saracen king Galafre claims Rome as his rightful heritage and is holding King Gaifier of Spoleto and his family as hostages. Galafre proposes to settle the matter by a judicial combat pitting a Saracen warrior against a Christian champion. After some hesitation, William agrees to face the powerful giant Corsolt on the battlefield. A lengthy and furious battle ensues, during which Corsolt slices off a piece of William's nose, thus earning for our hero the sobriquet "short-nosed William." Eventually William vanquishes the giant and wins his adversary's splendid horse, Alion. The Saracens are expelled, and a grateful King Gaifier offers his daughter in marriage to William. The wedding never occurs, however, because news arrives of Charlemagne's death and a new threat to King Louis's power (lines 150–1413).

A group of traitors plot to depose Louis and replace him with Acelin, son of Richard of Normandy. William and his men come to the rescue of the pitiful young king, who is in hiding in the city of Tours. William dispatches Acelin with a mighty blow to the head, and all of the traitors' supporters are slain or imprisoned, with the exception of the aged Richard of Normandy, whom William spares at the urging of the barons. William proceeds to secure Louis's authority in rebel territories throughout the kingdom. When the unrepentant Richard attempts to ambush William in Normandy, William defeats the traitor's forces and delivers Richard to the king, who imprisons him for life (lines 1414–2200).

Messengers arrive at Louis's court to announce that Guy the German has taken power in Rome and is claiming authority over the entire empire. The news prompts Louis to dissolve in tears, and William to assemble an army. Under Louis's command, the royal forces journey to Rome and set up camp. While William is engaged in a pillaging expedition, Louis's camp is attacked, and the terrified young king runs from one tent to another, frantically searching for William and his nephew Bertrand. They return in time to save the king and defeat Guy's forces. The conflict is definitively settled by a judicial combat between William and Guy. After vanquishing his opponent, William tosses the body into the Tiber and personally places the imperial crown on Louis's head (lines 2201–2623).

Louis returns to Paris, and William departs, hoping in vain for a bit of leisure. The faithful hero is soon summoned, however, to suppress a new rebellion. William defeats the rebels, ensures their allegiance to the king, and gives his sister in marriage to Louis. The narrator closes the story by declaring that the king, once secure in his power, has failed to show William proper gratitude (lines 2624–70).

Of the three poems, *The Coronation of Louis* is the oldest and the most overtly engaged in the politics of kingship. Like many chansons de geste, it contains a kernel of historical truth: in 813, a few months before his death, Charlemagne formally associated his son Louis with the throne.[21] However, the historical Louis differed significantly from the child depicted in the epic. Thirty-five years old at his first coronation, Charlemagne's successor was already King of Aquitaine and had a fair amount of military experience. Moreover, historical sources do not confirm the image of Louis as a weak and helpless sovereign. Far from being an accurate representation of Carolingian history, *The Coronation of Louis* appropriates distant events and personages in the interests of contemporary political concerns. In the early twelfth century, the Capetian monarchy was striving to establish itself as a dynastic institution. To this end, King Louis VI formally associated his eleven-year-old son Louis with the throne in 1131, in the presence of the pope. *The Coronation of Louis* implicitly conflates the two Louis in the epic imagination and makes a case for dynastic succession. The fictionalized son of Charlemagne is admittedly a pitiful figure, a "cowardly heir" (line 92) whose flaws are all the more evident in the wake of Charlemagne's idealized reign. Louis's survival depends on William's unwavering loyalty and tremendous prowess, reiterated with each new threat to the king's domain and authority. Paradoxically, however, Louis's very weakness supports the concept of hereditary monarchy. When William eliminates the powerful barons who attempt to disrupt peaceful succession, it becomes evident that political stability is guaranteed by the dynastic institution itself, not by the individual occupying the throne. William embodies the ideal of vassalic service, ensuring the preservation of royal authority and the royal domain even for a severely flawed sovereign.

Celebrated for his powerful arms ("Fierebrace") and easily recognized by his shortened nose, William defines himself primarily with respect to his distinguished lineage. Son of Aymeri of Narbonne and Hermenjart, he is ever conscious of his place in a network of siblings, nephews, and ancestors.[22] William is portrayed as both a champion of the crown and a defender of the Christian faith. Young and impetuous, he is known for his ferocity but also for his hearty laugh. Indeed, though to a lesser extent than the two succeeding poems, *The Coronation of Louis* introduces some comic elements into the narrative. When William beholds the traitor Hernaut of Orléans in the Royal Chapel in Aix, his pious intention to avoid killing his fellow man is abruptly undercut when he grabs Hernaut by the hair, strikes him on the neck, and then berates the dead man, exclaiming: "I sought only to frighten you a little / But you are dead, and I don't care a penny!" (lines 140–41).[23] A similar comic shift in register occurs after the fierce battle that has cost William part of his nose. When his nephews inquire anxiously if he is safe and unharmed, William replies in the affirmative, praising God and adding, "Except that my nose has been shortened a bit; / I surely don't know how it could be lengthened" (lines 1157–58).[24]

It is in this battle that William encounters one of his most memorable adversaries, the giant Saracen king Corsolt. The designation "Saracen" does not refer to any particular ethnic or religious group, but (like "pagan") tends to be associated with Muslim figures.[25] Either by design or through ignorance, Western medieval poets grossly misrepresent Islam and its adherents. Muslims are portrayed as idolaters who worship a trinity of gods, including the prophet Mohammed. They are exaggeratedly ugly and often demonic, as exemplified by the portrait of Corsolt:

Lez et anchés, hideus comme aversier;	Stout and cross-eyed, ugly as the devil;
Les eulz ot roges com charbon en brasier,	His eyes were as red as coals in a brazier,
La teste lee et herupé le chief;	His head was broad, his hair was bristly;
Entre .ii. eulx ot de lé demi pié,	There was a half-foot distance between his two eyes,
Une grant toise d'espaules au braier;	And a good six feet from his shoulders to his waist;

(lines 508–12)

Treacherous, duplicitous, and malevolent, the Saracens are at once a projection of Western anxieties and a foil for Christian heroes. Their moral and cultural otherness, used to justify Christian hegemony and "holy war" against Islam, does not preclude the presence of chivalric prowess and sentiment. Corsolt is a worthy adversary, quietly acknowledging William's valor and inflicting the emblematic wound that will become an indelible mark of William's identity. Corsolt's mighty blow is retold and commemorated in succeeding poems as evidence of William's sacrifice and extraordinary heroism in the face of seemingly insuperable odds.

THE CONVOY TO NÎMES

The Convoy to Nîmes, the shortest of the three texts, falls into three parts.[26]

On a beautiful spring day, William returns from a hunt and is met by his nephew Bertrand, who announces that King Louis has bestowed fiefs upon all of his barons—except William. Confronting the king directly, William recalls his exemplary service to Louis, fiercely enumerating his many deeds and sacrifices on behalf of the ungrateful monarch. While

Louis enjoys wealth and power, William is so destitute that he can barely feed his horse. Louis responds by offering William a series of recently vacated fiefs, all of which William angrily refuses on the grounds that they rightfully belong to the heirs of the deceased vassals. Louis then offers a quarter of his kingdom, but William again protests, refusing to be known as the vassal who deprived his lord of revenue. Prompted by a suggestion from Bertrand, William breaks the impasse by asking the king to grant him the right to conquer Spain, which in those days included the Muslim-held cities of Nîmes and Orange. After receiving permission to conquer these lands and hold them as Louis's vassal, William assembles an army of thirty thousand poor young knights hoping to secure their fortune while defending the Christian faith (lines 1–760).

William and his men depart, fully equipped with the liturgical objects and culinary utensils they will require in Saracen lands. As they approach Nîmes, they encounter a Saracen peasant driving a cart with a barrel full of salt. This prompts one of William's knights, Garnier, to devise a strategy reminiscent of the Trojan horse: William will requisition from the local peasantry a large number of carts, barrels, and oxen; the barrels will be filled with knights and weapons, then smuggled into Nîmes on the carts (lines 761–1069).

Disguised as a merchant, William leads the convoy into the city, where he and his men defeat the Saracens and assume control of Nîmes (lines 1070–1486).

The unflattering portrait of King Louis in the *Coronation* degenerates even further in *The Convoy to Nîmes,* which associates Charlemagne's ineffectual successor with the topos of royal ingratitude. Louis's transgression is twofold. By neglecting his most valuable and loyal vassal, he fails to reward the faithful service that William himself must recall in an angry litany of past exploits. And by offering William the lands of recently deceased vassals, Louis fails to recognize the hereditary nature of the fief, a principle largely accepted by the time the *Convoy* was composed and vigorously defended by William. The king's proposed remedy would merely sow internal conflict by disinheriting other faithful vassals. By contrast, the solution offered by Bertrand and William sidesteps the lack of available land (a very real problem in the twelfth century) and has transcendent value as a holy mission of reconquest. Indeed, at the end of his exchange with Louis, William reveals the true motive for his expedition. Having once observed "pagan devils" devastating land, burning churches, and attacking the Christian populace, he had tearfully vowed before God and St. Giles to free lands under Saracen rule.

Despite the seriousness of its territorial and spiritual concerns, *The Convoy to Nîmes* contains a strong dose of the humor that permeates the cycle as a whole. Cast in the heroicomic mode, the poem frequently juxtaposes epic grandeur with the mundane or the ridiculous. At the beginning of the narrative, William's legendary strength leads mainly to bothersome accidents. When he stomps into the royal palace, he strikes fear into the assembled barons by breaking his shoelaces; when he assumes a defiant stance before the king, he leans forcefully on his hunting bow and breaks it in two. The subsequent expedition to Nîmes exploits the comic potential of the disguise motif.[27] The noble Bertrand proves to be woefully incompetent in his role as a cart driver; when his cart sinks in the mud, the mishap is framed by solemn epic formulas typically associated with warfare. The valiant William, playfully posing as a wealthy merchant from Canterbury with eighteen children, appears as a short-term master of deception unable to repress his chivalric identity for long:

[Harpin] passa avant, si li tire la barbe,	[Harpin] came up to William and yanked on his beard,
Par un petit cent peus ne l'en errache;	Pulling out almost a hundred hairs.
Voit le Guillelmes, par un pou n'en enraige.	Seeing this, William nearly went out of his mind.
Lors dist Guillelmes, que ne l'entendi ame:	Then William grumbled without being heard:
"Por ce, s'ai ore mes granz sollers de vache	"Even though I'm wearing big leather shoes
Et ma gonele et mes conroiz si gastes,	And my clothes are in such bad shape,
Si ai ge non Guillelmes Fierebrace . . ."	I'm nonetheless called William Fierebrace . . ."

(lines 1332–38)

The poet modulates artfully between epic conflict and comic interlude, fashioning the hero as a formidable yet very human figure.

Although not based on an actual historical event, *The Convoy to Nîmes* is noteworthy for the precision of its geographical references. The accuracy of William's itinerary from Paris to Nîmes suggests that the poet was familiar with the Regordane Way used by both merchants and pilgrims in the Middle Ages.

THE CONQUEST OF ORANGE

The Conquest of Orange as it appears in the surviving manuscripts is likely a reworking of a lost, primitive version.[28]

After the exhilaration of conquering Nîmes, William has grown restless, having no minstrels or women to distract him and no Saracens to test his valor. His brief period of idleness is soon interrupted by the arrival of Gilbert of Lenu, who has escaped from a Saracen prison in Orange, a city ruled by King Aragon. When Gilbert describes the splendor of Orange and the extraordinary beauty of the Saracen queen Orable—wife of Tibaut of Africant and stepmother to Aragon—William resolves to possess both the lady and the city. Over the objections of his men, he persuades his nephew Guielin and the weary Gilbert to accompany him on a risky reconnaissance mission. Disguised as Saracen interpreters, the three men enter Orange and obtain an audience with Orable in her exotic tower of Gloriette (lines 1–737).

William's identity is soon exposed, and he and his companions defend themselves against a Saracen attack with the help of Orable, whose sympathies now lie with the Christian knights. She supplies them with armor, equipping William with her husband Tibaut's sword. The Saracens, however, manage to penetrate the tower by means of an underground passage. Thanks to Orable, who cleverly negotiates with Aragon, the three Christians are saved from immediate execution and thrown into prison. Orable informs them of a second underground passage that will allow Gilbert to return to Nîmes for reinforcements. When a Saracen overhears the plan, Orable is incarcerated with the Christian prisoners. Guielin cannot help teasing his uncle, insisting that the great William Fierebrace has become William the Lover. Eventually, William's nephew Bertrand arrives at the head of fifteen thousand troops to help William and Guielin defeat the Saracens. Bertrand slays Aragon, the Christians conquer Orange, and William liberates Orable, who converts to Christianity and takes the name Guibourc. She and William are married in a holy church that once served as a mosque (lines 738–1888).

There is evidence of a preexisting tradition attributing a conquest of Orange to William of Toulouse, our hero's historical prototype, who in fact made no such expedition. This legend appears to have been inspired by an earlier version of *The Conquest of Orange* that included more conventional epic material, including a siege of the city by Orable's husband Tibaut of Africant.[29] While its antecedents remain a matter of conjecture, the surviving poem is notable for its conjoining of epic conquest and amorous adventure, as well as its fascination with the exotic splendor of Islamic civilization. Woman, city, and treasure are intertwined through the reverberating sound of *or* (gold) embedded in proper names. Having sworn to capture **Or**ange and possess **Or**able, the most beautiful woman "from here to the **Or**ient" (line 203), Guillaume is delighted to find himself beside the lady in her tower of Gl**or**iette, on a bench encrusted with gold and silver. Orable thus appears as an eroticized commodity, a reflection of the material prestige associated with Muslim culture. When William and his companions first encounter her, she is the central figure in an exotic Oriental tableau:

A une part de la chambre leanz,	On one side of the interior chamber
Avoit un pin par tel esperiment	There was a pine tree with magical properties
. . . .	. . . .
La flor qu'en ist par est si avenant,	The flower it bears is magnificent,
Blanche est et inde et si est vermeillant.	White, blue, and crimson.
. . . .	. . . .
Pitre et canele, garingal et encens	Chrysanthemums, cinnamon, galangal, and incense
Flere soëf et ysope et piment.	Exhale sweet fragrances, along with hyssop and lemon balm.
La sist Orable, la dame d'Aufriquant;	There sat Orable, Tibaut of Africant's wife.
Ele ot vestu un paile escarinant.	She was dressed in a gown of Persian silk,
Estroit lacié por le cors qu'ele ot gent	The sides tightly laced up her beautiful body
De riche soie cousue par les flans.	With rich silk cord.

(lines 651–52, 655–56, 658–63)

The relationship between the Orient and sexuality is among the most persistent themes in Western literature, and it takes a particular form in the Old French epic, namely the Saracen Princess micro-narrative.[30] In this plot a Muslim princess falls in love with a Christian knight, perceives the flaws in her own religion, betrays her family, converts to Christianity, and marries the knight. She may be framed by an exotic décor, but her physical attributes correspond to Western ideals of female beauty. Blonde and fair-skinned, she is quickly de-exoticized and assimilated into her new Christian environment after baptism. Though Orable is cast from this mold, she is distinguished by her royal status and dignified comportment. She is instrumental in securing William's conquest, often appearing more resourceful than the hero himself. Orable is ultimately given a Christian name (**Gui**bourc) that echoes that of William (**Gui**llaume). Far from being absorbed by her male counterpart, however, she is a dominant figure in the cycle as a whole, and arguably one of the most powerful female characters in the Old French epic.

By casting William in the role of love-struck suitor, the poem raises provocative questions about genre and heroic identity. The once indomitable warrior adopts the language of courtly love lyric and undertakes an amorous quest, yet he resists the new epithet William the Lover. *The Conquest of Orange* admits some generic innovation to enrich William's heroic profile, but concludes by reinscribing the hero in a cycle of epic warfare which, the poet assures us, will occupy him daily for decades to come. The conquest of Orange henceforth becomes an integral part of William's name and heroic biography.

A Note on the Translation

The three poems presented here are already available in straightforward modern French translations designed to facilitate or replace the reading of the Old French originals.[31] While English versions do exist, no current volume provides an updated, accessible English translation of the three closely connected works.[32] Following the medieval manuscript tradition, our translation presents the works as a trilogy and strives to render the Old French assonanced decasyllabic verse into line-by-line standard modern English, capturing the sense of the original without attempting to preserve or imitate its formal properties. In almost all cases, we were able to render the elements present in the Old French line into the corresponding line of our translation, but on a few occasions we had to adjust the order of the original verses to accommodate the correct syntax of our translation.

Our translations are based on the critical editions of the *AB* redaction by Yvan G. Lepage, Duncan McMillan, and Claude Régnier.[33] In some fifteen instances, where readings from the other versions supplied missing information or offered a more coherent reading, we inserted a lower-case letter after the line number of the additional verse(s). The first instance of such a variation occurs in *The Coronation of Louis* at the end of the battle scene in which William kills Corsolt. We chose to insert two lines, 1139a and 1139b, from the *C* redaction because they provide necessary details about what William did after he found that Corsolt's sword was too long for him to strap on. Indeed, these lines—not present in the *AB* redaction—are necessary to the logic of this scene. Additional lines were added in ten places in *The Coronation of Louis* and three in *The Convoy to Nîmes*.

As we have seen, authors of chansons de geste of this period often used epic formulas as a strategy of repetition in their works. One of the formulas most frequently encountered in our works may be seen for the first time in line 1175 of *The Coronation of Louis*, "Guillelmes l'ot, si s'en rit volentiers," which we have rendered as "Hearing this, William laughed heartily." The formula occurs sixteen times in this form or in a very similar construction throughout the three poems presented here, and we translate it each time in the same words.

The monetary reference *denier* occurs occasionally in our texts. A denier is a basic silver coin of medieval France, worth about a nickel; twelve denier equal one sou. Since the denier has no modern equivalent, we have chosen to translate the term as "penny."

Finally, Old French verse of the period in question often employs binomial pairs in the same line. One example of this common practice occurs in line 1536 of *The Coronation of Louis* where the jongleur informs the audience that William "fu joianz et liez" (was joyful and happy). In another example from the *Coronation*, the poet particularly likes to pair the verb "to kill" (either *occire* or *tuer* in Old French) with a related term, usually *desmembrer* or *detranchier*, both meaning "to cut apart, dismember, tear to pieces." Examples can be found in lines 173, 588, 668, 737, 835, 1656, 1724, 2140, 2180, 2315, and 2334. This pairing is virtually absent from our other poems, although *The Conquest of Orange* has a triplet in line 1690: "slaughtered, killed, or slain." Medieval audiences were accustomed to this poetic approach, but the modern reader may find its usage a bit awkward. At the risk of seeming redundant, we have usually preserved binomial pairs in the same line in our translation to give the reader a more vivid sense of the original text.

Notes

1. This introduction owes much to Jones, *An Introduction to the Chansons de Geste,* 1–25, which contains a more detailed overview of the Old French epic.

2. Jones, *An Introduction to the Chansons de Geste,* 2.

3. See Duggan, "Medieval Epic as Popular Historiography."

4. The principal cycles are the Charlemagne cycle, the William of Orange cycle, the Doon de Mayence cycle (or Rebellious Baron cycle), and the Crusade cycle.

5. The medieval epic hero William of Orange, whose exploits are situated in the Carolingian period, is not to be confused with William I the Taciturn (1533–1584), Prince of Orange and leader of the Dutch revolt against the Spanish Hapsburgs, or King William III of England (1650–1702), also known as William of Orange.

6. Scholars have identified a number of secondary prototypes. See Corbellari, *Guillaume d'Orange,* 59–79.

7. There appears to have been some hesitation or confusion over the nature of William's distinctive nose. He is most often designated by his "court nez" (short nose), a deformity attributed to a battle injury in *The Coronation of Louis,* but that epithet may represent a distortion or rival of an original "corb nez" (crooked or hooked nose).

8. Garin of Monglane is William's great-grandfather, legendary ancestor of the illustrious lineage.

9. See Suard, *Guide de la chanson de geste,* 131–39; Tyssens, *La Geste de Guillaume d'Orange,* 153–62.

10. The surviving manuscripts fall into four principal redactions. *A*: BnF fr. 774 (A1); BnF fr. 1449 (A2); BnF fr. 368 (A3); Milan, Trivulziana 1025 (A4). *B*: Brit. Museum Royal 20 D XI (B1); BnF fr. 24369–24370 (B2). *C*: Boulogne-sur-Mer, Bib. Mun. 192. *D*: BnF fr. 1448. Also included in the *C* group is BnF nouv. acq. fr. 5094, a 38-line fragment of *The Coronation of Louis.* A fragmentary *E* redaction, Bern, Bib. de la Bourgeoisie 296, is missing *The Coronation of Louis, The Convoy to Nîmes,* and the beginning of *The Conquest of Orange.* For detailed information on the manuscript tradition, see the editions by Lepage, McMillan, and Régnier.

11. On the diffusion of Old French epic in Europe, see Suard, *Guide de la chanson de geste,* 363–84; Jones, *An Introduction to the Chansons de Geste,* 141–45. On the dissemination of the William of Orange material in particular, see Corbellari, *Guillaume d'Orange,* 189–234.

12. Assonance is understood here as the systematic repetition of the stressed vowel at the end of a line of verse. For example, cité, loer, and desvez share the stressed vowel /e/. Normally, a new laisse is marked by a change of assonance. Later epics tend to abandon assonance in favor of rhyme.

13. The following discussion of laisse technique is largely based on Rychner's seminal study of formulaic style in the Old French epic, *La chanson de geste: Essai sur l'art épique des jongleurs*, 68–125.

14. Quotations from *Le Couronnement de Louis*, *Le Charroi de Nîmes*, and *La Prise d'Orange* are from the editions by Lepage, McMillan, and Régnier, respectively. Translations are drawn from the present volume.

15. Rychner, *La chanson de geste*, 78.

16. Strictly speaking, only the end of laisse 26 fits into the series, while laisses 27 and 28 are "parallel" in their entirety.

17. *The Song of Roland* includes several series of laisses that are "similar" in their entirety. Most surviving instances of the device, however, do not mold the repeated action to the exact contours of each successive laisse. See Rychner, *La chanson de geste*, 100.

18. On formulaic style, see Rychner, *La chanson de geste*; Martin, *Les motifs dans la chanson de geste*; Heinemann, *L'art métrique de la chanson de geste*. Each of the studies presents formulaic composition from a different angle and with different classifications.

19. The definition of the epic formula has been debated at length. Following Rychner, we adopt the broad definition borrowed from Parry, "Studies in the Epic Technique of Oral Verse-Making. I. Homer and Homeric Style," 80; see Rychner, *La chanson de geste*, 147.

20. For a history of critical commentary on the text's compositional unity (or lack thereof), see Frappier, *Les chansons de geste du cycle de Guillaume d'Orange*, 2: 49–51, 113–20; Lachet, "Quelques échos."

21. On the historical context of *The Coronation of Louis*, see Collomp, "Le Couronnement de Louis et les tiroirs de l'histoire."

22. See Legros, "Le personnage de Guillaume," 165.

23. Legros, "Le personnage de Guillaume," 176.

24. On the comic mode in the William cycle, see Bennett, *Carnaval héroïque*.

25. There is an abundance of secondary literature on the representation of Islam in the chansons de geste. See, for example, Daniel, *Heroes and Saracens and Islam in the West*; Ramey, *Christian, Saracen and Genre*.

26. For a more detailed discussion of *The Convoy to Nîmes* and *The Conquest of Orange*, see Jones, *An Introduction to the Chansons de Geste*, 80–97.

27. See Suard, "Le motif du déguisement."

28. See Frappier, *Les chansons de geste du cycle de Guillaume d'Orange*, 2: 257–78.

29. Evidence of a preexisting legend includes the 1125 *Vita sancti Wilhelmi* (Life of St. William), which claims that William of Toulouse captured Orange from a certain Theobaldus during Charlemagne's reign. The hypothesis of a lost version of the *Conquest* is suggested by a number of allusions to the story in other songs of the William cycle that differ significantly from the extant poem. See Colby-Hall, "In Search of the Lost Epics."

30. Among the numerous studies devoted to the Saracen Princess, see Daniel, *Heroes and Saracens*, 69–93; de Weever, *Sheba's Daughters*; Kay, *The Chansons de Geste*, 25–48; Kinoshita, *Medieval Boundaries*, 46–73; Ramey, *Christian, Saracen and Genre*, 39–49.

31. *Le Couronnement de Louis*, trans. André Lanly; *Le Charroi de Nîmes*, ed. and trans. Claude Lachet; *La Prise d'Orange: Chanson de geste* (fin XIIe–début XIIIe siècle), ed. and trans. Claude Lachet; *Chansons de geste: Roland, Aimeri de Narbonne, Le Cou-*

ronnement de Louis, trans. Léon Clédat. Abridged versions appear in *Le Cycle de Guillaume d'Orange*, trans. Dominique Boutet.

32. All three texts are included in Glanville Price's 1975 English prose anthology titled *William, Count of Orange: Four Old French Epics*, but this volume is out of print and its language somewhat archaizing. See also Henri J. Godin's *Le Charroi de Nîmes: An English Translation with Notes*, also difficult to find and characterized by archaic language. *The Coronation of Louis* and *The Conquest of Orange* are included in other anthologies: both appear in Joan Ferrante's 1974 *Guillaume d'Orange: Four Twelfth-Century Epics*, a free-verse translation that attempts to reproduce Old French metrical patterns, and an assonanced verse rendering of the *Conquest* is included in Michael Newth's *Heroines of the French Epic: A Second Selection of Chansons de Geste*. See also the unpublished doctoral dissertation by Elizabeth P. Riggs, *La Prise d'Orange or William in Love: A Study and Translation of an Old French Epic of the William Cycle*, and Nirmal Dass's *The Crowning of Louis: A New Metrical Translation of the Old French Verse Epic*.

33. *Les Rédactions en vers du Couronnement de Louis*, ed. Yvan G. Lepage; *Le Charroi de Nîmes: Chanson de geste du XIIe siècle*, ed. Duncan McMillan, 2nd ed.; *Les Rédactions en vers de La Prise d'Orange*, ed. Claude Régnier, 2nd ed. On the quality of these editions, see Bennett, *The Cycle of Guillaume d'Orange or Garin de Monglane: A Critical Bibliography*, 69, 80, 123.

1

The Coronation of Louis

1.

Listen, lords, and may God the glorious
Help you by his commandment.
Would it please you to hear a worthy story,
Courtly and good, noble and agreeable?
I don't know why an ignoble jongleur[1] boasts,   5
Who doesn't say a single word until he's ordered to.
I shall not fail to sing to you about Louis
And short-nosed William the brave,
Who endured so much from the Saracens;
I don't believe anyone can sing to you of a better man.   10

2.

Lordly barons, would the lesson of a well-made
And agreeable song be pleasing to you?
When God chose ninety-nine realms,
The best was that of sweet France.

---

[1] A jongleur is an entertainer/performer, as often opposed to a trouvère, who is instead a composer (yet sometimes also the performer) of chansons de geste. Lines 5–6, which differ in subtle but important ways from manuscript to manuscript of the *Couronnement*, have posed significant difficulties of interpretation. Is the performer (or the author?) of this version of the poem criticizing all jongleurs in general as being unworthy, or just those who dare sing a rival version of this particular poem? Valuable critical studies of these lines can be found in Frappier, *Les Chansons de geste du cycle de Guillaume d'Orange*, 2: 60–64n, and Kullmann, "Le Prologue du *Couronnement de Louis* et le motif du vilain jongleur." Rather than choose a side, we have purposely left our translation as vague as the original.

Its greatest king was named Charlemagne; 15
He gladly exalted sweet France:
Every land God made bowed down to him.
He conquered Bavaria and Germany,
Normandy and Anjou and Brittany,
Lombardy and Navarre and Tuscany. 20

3.
The king who wears the golden crown of France
Must be courageous and brave in body;
If any man does him wrong,
The king must not evade danger in plains or woods
Until he has vanquished or killed him: 25
If it is not so, then France has lost its honor;
The story says he was wrongly crowned.

4.
When the chapel was consecrated at Aix
And the church was built and dedicated,
The court was good—you could see none finer; 30
Fourteen counts guarded the palace.
The destitute went there to find justice;
Everyone who pled his case was treated rightly.
In those days people did what was right, but that is no longer the
    case:
The wicked are all ruled by covetousness, 35
And lawful pleas have lost to bribes.
God, who rules and sustains us, is just;
The wicked will go to stinking hell,
The evil hole, from where they will not return.

5.
That day there were some eighteen bishops 40
As well as eighteen archbishops;
The pope of Rome sang the mass.
That day there was a most generous offering,
Such as was never seen greater in France;
The one who received it was a most worthy man. 45

6.

That day there were some twenty-six abbots,
As well as four crowned kings.
That day Louis was exalted
And the crown was placed upon the altar;
His father the king gave it to him that day.   50
An archbishop mounted the lectern
And preached to the Christians.
"Barons," he said, "listen to me:
Charlemagne is growing old
And can no longer fulfill his duties;   55
He has a son to whom he wishes to give the crown."
When they heard this, they were overcome with joy;
They all extended their hands toward God:
"Glorious Father, may you be thanked
That no foreign king is placed over us!"   60
Our emperor spoke to his son:
"Dear son," he said, "listen to me:
Behold the crown upon the altar;
I wish to give it to you, with these conditions:
Do not be evil or immoral or sinful,   65
Do not betray anyone,
Do not deprive the orphan of his lands.
If you agree, I shall praise the Lord God:
Take the crown and be crowned;
But if not, son, leave it there,   70
For I forbid you to touch it."

7.

"Louis, my son, look here at the crown:
If you take it, you are emperor of Rome;
You can easily lead eleven hundred men at arms,
Cross over the Gironde by force,   75
Defeat and destroy the pagan people;
And you must join their lands with ours.
If you wish to do this, I offer you the crown;
But if not, I shall never give it to you."

8.

"If, dear son, you accept bribes   80
And refuse to quell excessive pride,
Commit adultery or favor sinfulness,
Or deprive an orphan heir of his fiefdom,
Or take a single penny from a widow,
In the name of Jesus I forbid you this crown,   85
Son Louis, for you must not receive it."
The young man heard this but did not step forward.
Many a brave knight wept for him,
And the emperor was furious and irate:
"Alas," said he, "I've been deceived!   90
Some scoundrel lay beside my wife
And engendered this cowardly heir.
Never in his life will he be favored by me;
Were anyone to make him king, it would be a sin.
Now we shall have all his hair cut off;   95
He will be a monk in this monastery at Aix:
He will pull the ropes and be the sexton
And he will earn his food so he won't have to beg."
Beside the king sat Hernaut of Orléans,
A very proud and arrogant man,   100
Who began to address him with flattering words:
"Rightful emperor, calm down and hear me:
My lord is young, barely fifteen years old;
If he were knighted he would soon be killed.
Name me his regent, if you please,   105
For three years, and we shall see what comes of it;
If Louis decides to be a bold and good heir,
I'll return the crown to him gladly and willingly,
And I'll add to his lands and his fiefdom."
The king replied, "This should be granted."   110
—"Many thanks, my lord," said the flatterers,
Who were relatives of Duke Hernaut of Orléans.
He would already be king had William not arrived,
Who was returning from a hunt in the forest.
His nephew Bertrand ran to hold his stirrup.   115

He asked him, "Where are you coming from, fair nephew?"
—"In the name of God, my lord, from the church over there,
Where I heard a great wrong and a great sin;
Hernaut is trying to betray his rightful lord:
He is about to become king, for the Franks have so chosen."   120
—"It was an evil thought," said proud William.
With sword girded on, he entered the church
And pushed his way through the crowd before the knights.
He found Hernaut fully armed;
He had it in mind to cut off his head,   125
Until he remembered the glorious God in heaven,
And that it was a most grievous sin to kill a man.
He took his sword and put it back in its sheath,
Then strode forward once he had gathered himself;
He grabbed Hernaut by the hair with his left fist,   130
Raised the right one, and hit him on the neck;
He broke his chin right in two,
Striking him dead to the ground at his feet.
After he had killed him, he began to denounce him:
"Ha! foul wretch!" he said. "May God damn you!   135
Why did you seek to betray your rightful lord?
You should love him and hold him dear,
Increase his lands and augment his fiefs.
Flattery will never again avail you.
I sought only to frighten you a little,   140
But you are dead, and I don't care a penny!"
He saw the crown that was sitting on the altar;
The count seized it without a moment's delay,
Came to the youth, and placed it upon his head.
"Take it, fair lord, in the name of the God of heaven,   145
And may He give you strength to be a just ruler!"
The father saw this and was pleased for his son:
"Sir William, may you be profusely thanked:
Your lineage has exalted mine."

9.
"Ah, Louis," said Charles, "fair son,   150
You will have all my realm to hold.

You may keep it with these conditions:
That you never deprive a young heir of his rights
Nor take a penny's worth from a widow;
That you serve holy churches well   155
So that the devil can never shame you;
That you make your knights happy:
By them you will be honored and served,
And beloved and cherished through all lands."

10.
After they had made Louis king that day,   160
The discussion was over and the court departed.
Every Frenchman returned to his home.
Charles lived five more years and no more.
King Charles went up to the palace
And said to his son as soon as he saw him: 165

11.
"Louis my son, I'll not keep it from you:
You will have all my realm to rule
After my death, if God blesses me.
Whoever would fight me, I know he'll defy you;
Whoever hates me, I know he doesn't love you: 170
If I can capture him, by God the Son of Mary,
I won't consider any ransom at all,
But instead will have him cut to pieces and killed."

12.
"Louis my son, I don't care to keep it from you:
When God made a king to exalt his people,   175
He did not make him to render false judgment,
Nor to commit adultery and favor sinfulness,
Nor to deprive a young heir of his fief,
Nor take four pennies from a widow.
Instead, he must crush wrong beneath his feet,   180
Trample it under, break and obliterate it.
You must be humble before the poor,
And you must aid and advise them:

Teach them God's word for love of him.
You must be as steadfast against the proud   185
As a man-eating leopard;
And should anyone seek to declare war against you,
Send for the noble knights of France
Until you have more than thirty thousand.
Besiege him there where he seems strongest,   190
Laying waste and destroying all his land.
If you can capture or lay hands upon him,
Show no pity or mercy toward him,
But rather have him quartered,
Burned in a fire, or drowned in the sea.   195
For if the traitors saw you knocked to the ground
And had the chance to wage war on you,
The wicked flatterers and vile Norman cowards
Would immediately say:
'We had no use for such a king;   200
A hundred curses upon the head
Of anyone who goes to fight in his great army,
Or who goes to frequent his court!
We can help ourselves to his treasure.'
And I'd like to make you aware, if you wish, my son,   205
Of something else that will be of great use to you:
Do not make a lower-class man your advisor,
Neither a provost's nor an officer's son:
They will betray you for very little money.
But trust William the noble warrior,   210
Son of proud Aymeri of Narbonne,
Brother of Bernard of Brabant, the warrior;
And if they choose to aid and support you,
You can put complete trust in their service."
The youth replied, "You speak the truth, by my head."   215
He went to the count and fell at his feet.
Count William hastened to raise him up;
He asked him, "Young man, what do you want?"
—"In God's name, my lord, mercy and pity.
My father says you are a good knight,   220
That there is no baron like you under the cape of heaven;

I wish to place my lands and my fiefs in your care,
To guard them for me, noble knight,
Until I am able to receive my own armor."
The count replied, "Gladly, by my faith."   225
William swore to him by the saints of the church
That he would never possess four pennyworth,
Nor ever have a finger length nor half foot of anything,
Unless Louis had given it to him gladly and willingly.
Then he came to Charles, for he did not wish to delay;   230
He went to kneel before the king and said:
"Rightful emperor, I ask your leave,
For I must set off and ride
Straight to Rome to pray to St. Peter.
Some fifteen years past—I don't wish to hide it from you—   235
I promised to do so, but have been unable to;
I don't wish to postpone this voyage any longer."
Though angry and irate, the king consented,
Gave him forty knights,
And loaded thirty packhorses with gold and silver.   240
They hurried to kiss one another as he left.
The warrior swore not to return
Unless there were great difficulties;
Charles would be dead before his return,
With Louis still his heir.   245
Before William could do anything about it
Or return to France,
Louis would be falsely imprisoned and hidden away,
And all but cut to pieces;
William's delay could be fatal to him!   250

13.
William Fierebrace was in the church;
He asked leave of the emperor Charles,
Who gave him forty men at arms
And thirty packhorses laden with gold and silver.
The count departed without delay,   255
And Louis escorted him with a great crowd;
In tears, he called to William Fierebrace:

"Ah, noble count, for God in heaven,
Behold my father who is leaving this world:
He is old and feeble and will not bear arms again,   260
While I am young and immature;
If I don't have help, things will go badly!"
The count replied, "Do not be uneasy,
For, by the apostle they worship at the monument,[2]
Once I have made this pilgrimage,   265
And you send for me by sealed letters
Or by a very trustworthy man,
There is no one I can imagine who will prevent me
From rescuing you with my powerful band of men."
The count departed without any delay.   270
I do not know what I should tell you about his trip:
With wearisome effort Fierebrace crossed
The Saint Bernard Pass and reached Rome.

14.
Noble and valiant William departed,
Along with Guielin and illustrious Bertrand.   275
Beneath their capes they carried engraved swords,
And even so they had donned
Their good hauberks and gilded helms.
The squires were extremely weary
From carrying their strong shields and lances.   280
I do not know what to tell you about their trip:
They crossed the Saint Bernard Pass, which wearied them greatly,
And rode through the region around Rome,
Not stopping until they reached that city.
The squires secured lodgings;   285
Their host, named Cirtaige,
Gathered together all he possessed.
That night the count was well provided for.
After dinner they went to rest;
The count, who was quite fatigued, slept.   290

---

2   Old French *arche* refers here, as well as in line 496, to the funeral monument of St. Peter in the
Vatican, built directly over the tomb of the first pope. See Lefèvre, "L'*arche* de Saint-Pierre de Rome
dans le *Couronnement de Louis.*" And cf. note to line 444.

He dreamt a dream that greatly frightened him:
From Russia there came a blazing fire
That consumed Rome in all directions;
A swift, fierce hound came running ahead,
Separated from the others;   295
William was beneath a branching tree;
He was most frightened by this beast,
Because it gave him such a blow with its paw
That he was struck to the ground.
The count awakened and commended himself to God.   300
No dream ever proved more truthful,
For Saracens were on the march.
King Galafre and King Tenebrez,
King Cremus and Emir Corsolt
Had captured the main keep at Capua.   305
King Gaifier has been imprisoned there,
He, his daughter, and his beautiful wife,
Along with thirty thousand prisoners
Whose heads were to be separated from their bodies.
God so loved courageous William   310
That he was able to free them from prison
By defeating Corsolt from across the Red Sea,
The strongest man anyone had ever heard of.
He cut short William's nose,
As you will hear before night falls,   315
If you pay me enough that I'll want to sing.[3]
Not long afterwards dawn broke:
Count William arose early
And went to attend services in the church.
He had all his armor placed upon the altar;   320
He intended to redeem it later with Arabian gold.
The pope was most noble and valiant:
He put on his vestments to sing the mass.
When the service was over and ended,
Behold two messengers riding rapidly!   325

---

3   Direct addresses to the listening public by the jongleur, especially those requesting money,
are a staple of oral style in Old French chansons de geste. They often mark significant breaks in the
narration, as here.

They will soon recount such news
As made many a good man angry that day.

15.
William Fierebrace was in the church.
The learnèd pope had sung the mass;
When he had finished, two messengers came   330
To him bearing bitter news:
The Saracens are causing him much harm;
They have taken by force the strong city of Capua
And captured wise Gaifier of Spoleto
Along with thirty thousand prisoners;   335
If they are not helped, all will die by the sword.
The pope—a very kind man—
Asked after William Fierebrace.
They pointed him out down on the marble floor
Praying to God, the heavenly Father,   340
To give him strength and honor and men,
As well as to his lord Louis, the son of Charles.
The pope did not hesitate at all;
He took a staff and tapped him on the shoulder:
The count stood up and looked straight at him.   345

16.
Count William rose to his feet,
And the pope began to address him:
"Ah, noble sir, in the name of the righteous God,
Tell me if you can help me.
Pagans and devils are attacking us now,   350
And are headed by King Galafre.
The king who used to help us is destroyed:
They have captured King Gaifier,
As well as his daughter and noble wife,
Along with thirty thousand wretched prisoners.   355
If they are not helped, they will all lose their heads."
—"Ah, God, help us!" said proud-faced William.
For fear of so many kings he began to cross himself;
His nephew Bertrand started to speak to him:

"Uncle William, are you mad?   360
I've never before seen you afraid of any man."
—"Mercy, for God's sake, fair nephew," William replied,
"Our strength is nothing against theirs.
Instead, we must find a messenger
And send him to Louis,   365
Urging him to come to aid and rescue us.
Let Charles stay behind to assure justice:
He is old and frail and can no longer ride."
Bertrand replied, "May the righteous God
Overwhelm and drive mad and kill   370
Anyone who would ever carry this message,
And may his shield be pierced and shattered,
And his hauberk shredded and frayed,
And may he himself by struck by a stout lance,
So that they can recognize him for a messenger!   375
Hundreds and thousands of pagans are attacking us;
To arms, quickly, there is no time for delay!
Let us defend ourselves without hesitation."
The Romans were frightened:
They were few in number, less than a hundred thousand.   380

17.
Proud-faced William was in the church.
The pope, who was courtly and wise, said,
"Noble sir, for God in heaven,
Please save us from this savage people."
—"Ah, God, help us!" said Count Fierebrace,   385
"I have come to make my pilgrimage,
Bringing only a very small band of men;
I have but sixty armed knights
And cannot combat so many kings."
—"Ah, God, help us!" said the wise pope.   390
"Behold St. Peter here, protector of souls;
If you fight in his name today, my lord,
You can eat meat all the days of your life
And have as many women as you desire;
No sin you commit will be so grievous,   395

As long as you can avoid treason,
That it will not be pardoned in your lifetime.
You will be lodged in paradise,
For our Lord helps his dear friends:
St. Gabriel will be your guide."   400
—"Ah, God, help us!" said Count Fierebrace,
"No cleric ever had a more generous heart!
Now nothing will prevent me—no man I know
Or no pagan, however wild or cruel—
From going to combat these scoundrels!   405
Fair nephew Bertrand, go take up your weapons,
Along with Guielin and the other men-at-arms."
William Fierebrace demanded armor;
It was brought into the square before him.
He put on the hauberk, laced up the green helm,   410
And girded on the sword by its silken straps.
They brought his warhorse to him in the square;
The count mounted without anyone holding his stirrup.
A red shield hung at his neck;
In his hand he held a stiff sharp-edged spear   415
To which a gonfalon was attached by five golden nails.
"Your excellency," said wise William,
"How many men do you have in your borderlands?"
The pope said, "I shall tell you without fail:
We are three thousand, all with ventail   420
And strong spear and sharp-edged sword."
The count replied, "That's a good start.
Have them armed, along with all the foot soldiers,
Who can hold the gates and barriers for us."
—"It is right to do so," he replied.   425
From throughout Rome they came.
When they were armed and all in place,
The pope blessed them with the sign of the cross:
"Lordly barons," said the learnèd pope,
"Whoever dies this day in battle   430
Will be lodged in paradise,
For our Lord helps his dear friends;
St. Gabriel will be his guide."

Then they stood up; each one took up his arms
Against the haughty and savage people.   435
When they were about to pass through the main gate,
Which was not low, toward the ships,
The wise pope said, "Lordly barons,
Keep these men at arms here.
I shall go speak to the pagan emir   440
To see if I can promise him enough money
To turn back his ships and launches,
Along with his large army on these river banks.
I shall give him the entire papal treasure[4]—
There will not remain a chalice or cope,   445
Gold or silver, or anything worth a penny—
Rather than have so many wise and noble men die."
And they replied, "It is good to know this."
With that the pope set off, accompanied by an abbot;
He did not stop until he reached the tent   450
Where he found the powerful emir Galafre;
He did not greet him, as it was not right to do so.
The mighty king looked proudly at him;
The pope immediately addressed him:
"My lord," he said, "I am a messenger here   455
From God and St. Peter, who watches over souls.
On his behalf I wish to give you a message
To return to your ships and your launches,
Along with your mighty host, which is lined up here.
I shall give you the entire papal treasure;   460
There will not remain a chalice or cope,
Gold or silver, or anything worth a penny,
Rather than have so many noble men at arms die.
Take counsel, noble and well-born king."
The king replied, "You are not very wise.   465
I have come here into my rightful inheritance,
Won by my ancestors, my forebears,
By Romulus and Julius Caesar,

---

4   Old French *arche,* here and at line 460, refers to the papal treasure that was kept in large coffers
so as to be easily moveable in case of attack.

Who built these walls, these towers, and these barricades.
If I can lay ruin to this palace by force, 470
I shall destroy everything that belongs to your God:
His clerics who serve him in shame and sadness."
The pope was most frightened and would not
Have wished to be there for all the gold of Carthage.
He asked Emir Galafre for passage, 475
And he gave him three Saracens for safe conduct.
King Galafre addressed him further:
"Speak to me, you with the wide-brimmed hat:
Do not say that I do you any wrong
Regarding the city that is my inheritance; 480
Choose a man skilled in arms,
And I'll have one of very high lineage:
We shall put them in the square as our champions;
If your God is powerful enough
That my champion be defeated in arms, 485
Then you will have won Rome as your inheritance;
In all your days you'll not find anyone
To take anything from you, even so little as a cheese.
And if I should fail to keep my word to you,
Retain my two sons as hostages[5] 490
And hang them both from a tree,
For not even a penny could ransom them."
When the pope heard these wise words,
He could not have been happier for all the wealth of Carthage;
At once he thought of Count Fierebrace, 495
Whom he had armed in the church before the monument.
He was well aware that no one could bear arms better.

18.
The pope was very well informed;
He saw clearly now that God wished to help them,

---

5   In the chansons de geste, hostages were often used to guarantee an agreement or serve as
pledges for judicial combat. They could be punished with death if the agreement were broken
or if their champion were defeated. It is generally believed that such extreme measures did not
correspond to twelfth-century legal practices, but were rather examples of epic exaggeration. See
also lines 2016, 2415, and 2440.

Since by a single man his rights could be defended.   500
He clearly claimed his rights before the enemy:
"Sire," he said, "I don't wish to hide it from you:
Since two men alone can decide our case,
I would willingly see your champion
Who wishes to challenge God for Rome."   505
The king replied, "I am quite relieved."
King Corsolt was brought before him,
Stout and cross-eyed, ugly as the devil;
His eyes were as red as coals in a brazier,
His head was broad, his hair was bristly;   510
There was a half-foot distance between his two eyes,
And a good six feet from his shoulders to his waist;
An uglier man could not live on bread.
He began to roll his eyes in the direction of the pope
And shouted, "Little man, what do you want?   515
Are you shaved so bald for some religious reason?"
—"Sir," he answered, "in church I must serve
St. Peter and God, who rules over us.
On his behalf I wish to urge you
To make your armies turn back: 520
I shall give you the church's treasure—
Not a censer or chalice will remain,
Not a penny's worth of gold or silver:
All will be ready there for you outside."
The king replied, "You are not very smart   525
To dare plead so before us!
Your God is the one who's made me the angriest ever:
He killed my father with a lightning bolt:
He was consumed by fire, no one could save him.
After God burned him up, he did a smart thing: 530
He rose to heaven and chose not to return here.
I could not follow or pursue him,
But I took vengeance on his people afterwards:
Of those who were baptized over the fonts,[6]

---

6   Corsolt is referring to Christians. The Old French term is *lever*, which designates the practice
of lifting an individual over the baptismal font.

I had more than thirty thousand killed,   535
Burnt in fire, and drowned in water.
Since I could not combat God up there,
I didn't want to leave any of his people here below,
And God and I have nothing more to fight about:
The earth is mine and the heavens will be his.   540
If I can take this earthly realm by force,
I'll have whatever belongs to God destroyed
And the clerics flayed alive with knives.
And yourself, as head of the church,
I'll have you burned over charcoals in a grill,   545
So that your liver will fall into the brazier!"
When the pope heard him speak in this manner,
It is no wonder he was frightened.
He and the abbot consulted among themselves:
"By St. Denis, this Turk is insane!   550
It's a great wonder he still has earth beneath his feet
And that God hasn't sent him to hell's fire,
Or that the ground hasn't caved in beneath him.
Oh! William, proud-faced marquis,
May the Judge of the world protect you!   555
Your strength is nothing compared to his."
The pope requested safe-conduct from proud Galafre,
And he gave him his wife's sons,
Who led him on foot as far as Rome.
Count William was first to come forward;   560
He grabbed the iron of his stirrup:
"My lord," he said, "how did it go?
Tell me, please: did you see the devil
Who wants to challenge God for possession of Rome?
Noble sir, did you make it that far?"   565
—"Yes, fair sir, I don't wish to hide it from you:
It is not a man, but rather a devil.
If Roland and Olivier were alive,
Yvon and Yvoire, Haton and Berangier,
And the archbishop, and the young Manessier,   570
Estot of Langres, and courtly Gaifier,
As well as Gautier and Angelier,

The Twelve Peers, who were slain,
And if Aymeri the warrior were here,
Your good father, who was a fine knight,   575
And all your brothers, who are most praiseworthy,
None would dare face him in battle."
—"My God!" said William, "tell me what will happen!
I see clearly that the clergy is corrupt:
You used to say that God is so powerful   580
That anyone he wishes to support and help
Would never afterwards be disgraced or shamed
And never burned in fire or drowned in the sea.
But by the apostle they venerate in Rome,
Even if he were a hundred feet tall,   585
I would still fight him with iron and steel.
If God chooses to debase our religion,
I could well be killed and dismembered;
But if he wishes to support and help us,
No man under heaven could defeat me,   590
Burn me in a fire, or drown me in the sea."
When the pope heard him speak in this manner:
"Oh!" he said, "noble knight,
May He who was raised on the cross protect you!
No knight ever spoke bolder words.   595
May God help you wherever you go,
Since you have Him in your mind and heart!"
He carried St. Peter's arm out of the church,
Had the gold and silver stripped off it,
And they made the count kiss its main joint.   600
Then they made the sign of the cross over his banded helm,
Across his heart, and both front and back.
These relics were to help him that day:
There was no man who could wound him,
Not even as deeply as two pennies are thick,   605
For which the noble count was later much blamed.
Soon afterwards he remounted his powerful warhorse,
Hung a quartered shield from his neck,
And held his strong slashing spear in his fist.
He did not stop until he reached the knoll.   610

Pagans and Saracens watched him carefully,
Saying to one another, "This is a handsome knight,
Brave and wise, courtly and learnèd;
If he were battling someone his equal,
It would be a fierce fight from the start;   615
But he won't have a chance against Corsolt,
Who wouldn't give a penny for fourteen like him."

19.
King Galafre came out of his tent;
He was dressed and shod like a king;
He looked toward the knoll and the knight upon it   620
And said to his men, "The Frenchman has come;
I see him upon the knoll; his shield suits him well.
He must do battle against muscular Corsolt,
But he is so small and slight in comparison.
Mohammed and Cain will be worth nothing   625
If this knight is not vanquished by Corsolt."
The king called for Corsolt and he came to him;
He went toward him with both arms extended:
"Fair nephew," he said, "you are most welcome!
Behold the Frenchman up there on the knoll: 630
If you challenge him, he will refuse to budge."
Corsolt replied, "He is defeated and dead!
Since I see him, I won't wait any longer.
Bring me my armor, let there be no delay!"
Seven kings and fifteen dukes rushed   635
To bring him his arms beneath a branching tree;
I don't think there was ever any finer armor:
If any other man had put them on his back,
He could not have budged for all the gold that ever was.

20.
Fourteen kings armed the devil;   640
On his back they placed a steel byrnie,
Over the byrnie a white padded hauberk,
Then they strapped on the sharp steel sword:
It was six feet long and a half foot wide;

He had laced on his bow and quiver;   645
He had his crossbow and his steel knife,
And sharpened bolts, readied to launch.
They brought him his warhorse Alion—
The horse was marvelously high-spirited:
So wild, as I've been told,   650
That no one dared get closer than six feet to it,
Not even someone it was accustomed to.
Four javelins were attached to his saddle,
And iron maces to the back of the seat;
King Corsolt mounted by the stirrup   655
And hung a quartered shield from his neck;
The shield had over six feet of pure gold,
But he would not accept a bow or lance.
They dressed him well in padded armor.
My God! how he could master his steed: 660
He made the horse run so fast
That neither hare nor greyhound could keep up!
He began to address his uncle,
Shouting, "Be quiet; listen to me!
Have the seneschal summoned at once,   665
The tables set, the food prepared.
I have to ride forth to meet this Frenchman:
I'll have killed him and cut him to pieces
Faster than one can cover a half acre by foot!
I won't deign to touch him with my sword   670
If I can strike a blow with my mace.
If I don't immediately strike down him and his horse,
May a noble never again offer me a thing to eat!"
The pagans exclaimed, "May Mohammed help you!"
He began to ride right through the army;   675
They commended him to Mohammed, whom he held dear.
Count William saw his enemy approaching,
Ugly, hideous, and weighed down with armor;
No one need doubt that he was frightened;
He called upon God, the righteous Father: 680
"Holy Mary, what a splendid horse!
It's a most worthy steed to help its worthy rider;

I must spare it any blows;
May God, who judges all, protect it
So that I not harm it with my sword!"   685
A coward would never use such words.

21.

William was mounted upon the knoll,
Turned out and dressed in beautiful armor.
He saw the frightful pagan approaching
And could not be blamed if he feared him.   690
He dismounted from his swift horse;
He had turned his face toward the east,
And he pronounced a most effective prayer;
Beneath the heavens was no man born of woman
Who, if he prayed it with good will   695
In the morning upon arising,
Could ever be overwhelmed by devils.
He called upon God with great humility:[7]
"Glorious Father, who caused me to be born,
You made the earth according to your will   700
And closed it all around by the sea;
You formed Adam and then Eve, his equal,
And led them into paradise to dwell;
The fruit of all the trees was given them,
Except a single apple tree that was forbidden;   705
They ate of it, which was great folly,
And were greatly shamed when they could not hide it.
They had to leave paradise,
Come down to earth, dig and work the ground,

---

7   This is the first of three epic credos in the poems in this volume (also at lines 977–1029, and
CO lines 804–17), a stylized prayer in which a Christian hero in extreme danger calls upon God
and the saints to watch over and spare him, following a codified structure. In the first and longest
part he invokes episodes from the Old and New Testaments to show how God has come to the aid
of his people—in this case, principally the Creation story and Fall of Adam and Eve; Noah and
the flood; the birth, life, death, and resurrection of Jesus. Next he expresses his faith through the
formula "Just as all this is true," then ends his prayer by requesting God's saving protection. The
classic study is that by Labande, "Le credo épique: À propos des prières dans les chansons de geste."
See also Frappier, Les Chansons de geste du cycle de Guillaume d'Orange, 2: 131–40; Rossi, "La prière
de demande dans l'épopée"; Roussel, Conter de geste au XIVe siècle, 306ff.

And suffer and endure this mortal life.   710
Cain in his cruelty killed Abel,
And the earth itself wept and cried out;
On that day it was given a cruel gift:
Nothing sprang from it that did not have to return to it.
God! You caused all those descended   715
From these two people to die in the flood
At the time of the ark; this is the truth.
Noah was the only one to escape,
With his three sons and their wives.
In order to restore the world, from all the animals   720
He had a male and female placed in the ark.
Lord God, from the people descended from them
Came forth the Virgin full of grace,
In whom you deigned to become incarnate.
Your body too was made of flesh and bone   725
And of holy blood that was claimed by martyrdom.
In the wonderful city of Bethlehem,
Fair Lord, you were pleased to be born,
Precisely on the night of Noel.
St. Anastasia was to hold you over the baptismal font;   730
She had no hands to do you the honor,
But you restored them to her according to her wish.
You were visited by the three kings,
With gold and myrrh and pure incense;
You had them leave by a different route,   735
Because of Herod who was so cruel
That he wanted to have them killed and dismembered.
The Holy Innocents were decapitated—
Eighty thousand, according to the learnèd clerics.
For thirty-two years you traveled the earth   740
Like any other man, teaching the people;
You went into the desert to fast
For a full forty days and nights,
And let yourself be tormented by the devil.
On Palm Sunday, when one must carry palms,   745
It pleased you, true God, to enter
Jerusalem, the splendid city,

Through Gates of Gold, which they opened.
You abandoned the rich, it is true,
And turned your heart to the destitute. 750
The leper was living at Simon's house
And the twelve apostles were gathered there;
Mary Magdalene secretly crept
Beneath the table, without speaking a word,
Washed your two feet with her precious tears, 755
And afterwards wiped them with her hair;
Her sins were immediately forgiven her.
In Jerusalem Judas betrayed you cruelly,
Selling you in his great folly,
For thirty pennies from the time of Methuselah; 760
With a kiss he turned you over to the false Jews
And you were tied and secured to the stake
Until morning, when dawn broke,
When they had you taken to a knoll,
Mount Calvary, as I have heard it called. 765
They made you carry your heavy cross on your shoulders,
Dressed in a most hideous tunic.
You did not advance a step, in truth,
Without being struck or wounded.
Your body was tortured on the holy cross 770
And your dear arms and legs worn and wounded.
Longinus came, a most fortunate man;
He could not see you, but heard you speak,
And with his lance struck you in the side;
Blood and water flowed down into his hands, 775
He rubbed his eyes and immediately saw the light;
He begged for mercy in great humility
And his sins were immediately pardoned.
Nicodemus, along with Joseph,
Came stealing up like practiced thieves: 780
They took down your limbs from the cross
And placed and deposited them in the tomb.
On the third day you rose again as God
And descended straight into hell;
You brought forth all your friends, 785

Who had been there for a long while.
Just as all this is true, dear God of majesty,
Defend my body that I not be harmed,
For I must do combat against this evil one,
Who is so tall, so enormous, and so muscular.   790
Holy Mary, if it please you, help me,
May I not show any cowardice in my weakness,
That might cast blame upon my lineage."
He crossed himself and stood up.
The Saracen came toward him fully armed   795
And spoke to William where he saw him:
"Tell me, Frenchman, and don't hide it:
To whom were you speaking at such length?"
—"Truly," said William, "you will now hear the truth:
To the God of glory, the King of majesty,   800
Who through his goodness helps me
That I may cut off all your limbs
And defeat you on the field of battle."
—"That is madness," said the pagan.
"So do you think that your God has the power   805
To protect you against me on the field of battle?"
—"Foul wretch," said William, "May God damn you!
Because if he wishes to sustain and protect me,
Your great arrogance will soon be broken."
—"Truly," said the Turk, "that's a most haughty thought!   810
If you agree to adore Mohammed
And abandon and disavow your God,
I would give you wealth and riches
More than ever your forebears had."
—"Foul wretch," said William, "May God damn you!   815
I will never disavow my God."
—"Truly," said the Turk, "you are quite haughty
When you refuse to refrain from battle.
What is your name? Don't hide it from me."
—"My name is William the marquis, so help me God,   820
Son of Aymeri, the old white-bearded one,
And bright-faced Hermenjart is my mother;
My brothers are Bernard of the city of Brabant,

Garin, who is most worthy of praise,
Beuve the feared, of Commarchis,   825
Guibert of Andernas, the firstborn;
And Aymer the woebegone is also my brother,
Who never takes shelter or celebrates
But is always out in the wind and rain
Killing Saracens and Slavs;   830
He can never love your people!"
The pagan heard this, and nearly went mad;
He rolled his eyes and raised his eyelids:
"Vile Frenchman, you have lived too long,
For you have slaughtered and destroyed my lineage."   835

22.

The Saracen spoke to him haughtily:
"Say there, William, you are very stupid
To believe in someone who can't help you at all.
God is up there, beyond the firmament;
He's never possessed even an acre here on earth,   840
It is under Mohammed's command instead.
I have no more esteem for all your masses
And your sacraments, your marriages
And your engagements, than I do for a passing breeze.
Christianity is total foolishness."   845
—"Foul wretch," replied William, "May God destroy you!
Your religion is worth nothing
Because Mohammed, everyone knows,
Was a prophet of Almighty God.
He came to earth, as many people know,   850
And came to Mecca first of all,
But he drank too much in his inebriation,
Then filthy pigs devoured him.[8]
Anyone who believes in him doesn't have good sense!"

---

8 Medieval Christian apologists—among many others Gerald of Wales, Alan of Lille, and
Matthew Paris—frequently allude to a "shameful death" suffered by the Prophet, in opposition
to Christ's saintly one. In this totally fanciful account, he was eaten by dogs and/or suffocated and
eaten by pigs while he was in a drunken stupor. See Daniel, *Islam and the West*, 102–7.

The pagan said, "You are a dirty liar.   855
If you agree to do all I ask
And believe truly in Mohammed,
I shall give you more wealth and land
Than all your forebears ever had.
For you are descended from very noble people;   860
I have often heard tell of your mighty deeds;
It would be a great loss were you to die ignobly here.
If you agree to this, tell me at once,
Or if not, you will swiftly die!"
—"Foul wretch," said William, "May God destroy you!   865
Now I esteem you less than I did at first:
Threats show a lack of courage."
William mounted most adroitly,
Without using the stirrup or grasping the saddle horn.
He took his shield and hung it from his neck;   870
He brandished his spear so angrily
That the shaft and the banner on it shook.
The Saracen looked intently at him
And said softly, so as not to be overheard:
"By Mohammed, to whom my soul belongs,   875
This man is full of mighty courage."
Had William known his wishes
And that he wanted to reach an accord,
He would have found peace easily.

23.
"Say there, Frenchman," said savage Corsolt,   880
"For your God, for whom you are about to fight,
Do you claim any heritage in Rome?"
—"You will hear at once," said Count Fierebrace:
"I am about to fight armed and on horseback
In the name of God, the heavenly Father.   885
Rome rightly belongs to our emperor Charles—
Tuscany and all the area around Rome;
St. Peter is the bridge and gateway,
And the pope who guards it for him."
The Turk replied, "You are not very wise   890

To want to claim the heritage by force,
For then you have no choice but to attack me.
Now I shall give you a great advantage:
Take your lance and hold tight to your weapon,
Strike me on the shield—I won't move it: 895
I want to see a bit of your strength,
What a little man can do in battle."
And William said, "I'd be a fool to wait any longer."
He spurred his horse, crossed an acre
Of the high, broad mountain. 900
He gripped his weapons tightly to himself;
The Saracen did not move from his place.
The pope said, "Now we shall witness a battle!
Fall to your knees, every one of you,
And pray to God with all your heart 905
That he bring William Fierebrace back to us
Safe and sound within the confines of Rome."
The noble count saw the good people
Praying for him; he would be a fool to wait any longer.
He spurred his steed and let fall the reins; 910
He brandished his lance with its silken banner,
Struck the pagan in the middle of his shield,
Piercing through the gold, the varnish and the wood;
He smashed and destroyed his hauberk,
His old byrnie was not worth a piece of straw; 915
William's strong spear penetrated his body
So far that one could hang a cape over the iron
That came through, if one were paying attention.
Count William passed mightily by,
Pulling his good spear out of Corsolt's body. 920
The pagan never lost his seat,
But said softly, so no one could know:
"By Mohammed, to whom I've sworn homage,
One is a great fool to mock a small man
When he sees him enter the field of combat! 925
When I saw him this morning on the glade
I cared little for him or his men,
And to be sure it was great folly

To give him the advantage over me,
For I've never before been so injured by any man." 930
He was in such pain that he nearly fainted.
Count William hurried to strike him again.

24.
William was very powerful and strong;
He struck the pagan through his body,
Pulled the iron out with such great vigor 935
That he ripped the gorget from his neck,
And his good golden shield fell to the ground.
All the Romans cried out loudly:
"Strike again, noble sir, God is with you!
St. Peter, my lord, be a guarantor for our side!" 940
Count William heard these words;
He spurred his steed, which sprang forward at once,
Brandished his spear, unfurled his banner,
Struck the pagan's hauberk on his back,
Smashing, tearing open, and breaking it; 945
His old byrnie was not worth two nails:
William thrust his spear right through his body,
Such that the iron came out the other side.
Another man would have died from a lesser wound.
The pagan did not even flinch: 950
He took a javelin from his saddlebow
And threw it at William so hard
That it sounded like a thunder clap.
The count, afraid of being killed, ducked,
And the missile struck the armor on his shoulder; 955
God protected him so that it did not strike flesh.
"God," said the count, "who formed St. Lot,
Defend me, Lord, that I not die yet."

25.
The Saracen felt gravely wounded:
William's good spear lay next to his lung 960
And his blood was flowing down to his spur;
He said softly, so no one could hear:

"By Mohammed, whose mercy I await,
No man ever before did me such harm.
And to be sure I was very stupid   965
To offer him the first blow against me!"
The evil wretch grabbed a sharp dart
And threw it forcefully at William;
The blow sounded like an eagle in flight:
The count ducked for fear of the rascal,   970
But it split his lion-emblazoned shield;
His old byrnie was of no avail:
It passed beside him with such force
That it struck the sand two feet beyond.
William saw this and bowed his head,   975
Beseeching God by his holy name:
"Glorious Father, who formed all the world,
Who made earth upon a marble cornerstone
And closed it all around with the salt sea,
Who made Adam of earth and mud,   980
Eve his wife, as we know for certain,
And gave them the gift of paradise
And the fruit of all the trees,
Except that of a single apple tree;
They ate from it, a most wicked deed,   985
But then were punished severely:
They went to hell, the pit of Baratron,
Who was served by Beelzebub and Nero.
One Easter season, in procession,
You rode upon the ass's babe   990
And were followed by little children;
On Palm Sunday the priests and novices
All processed together.
And you took lodging with the leper Simon.
You forgave the Magdalene,   995
Who laid her eyes upon your feet
And wept with true contrition;
You raised her up by her chin
And pardoned her sins.
There Judas betrayed you: 1000

He sold you, for which he was punished,
The wicked one received thirty pennies.
You were nailed to the cross:
The Jews behaved like wicked traitors;
They did not want to believe in your Resurrection. 1005
You rose to heaven on the day of the Ascension;
My Lord, the great redemption will come
At the judgment, where we will all gather.
There a father will be worth no more than his son,
Even the priest will not precede the novice, 1010
Nor the archbishop his little servant,
Nor king before duke, nor the count the merchant.
And you confessed the apostles.
You made St. Peter the head of Nero's Meadow[9]
And converted his companion St. Paul; 1015
You saved Jonah from the whale's belly,
Pardoned Mary Magdalene,
Saved Daniel from the lion's den;
You outwitted evil Simon Magus;
Moses saw the fire within the bush 1020
That did not consume or char it.
Just as all this is true, and one must believe it,
Defend me from shame or capture
And do not let this wicked Saracen kill me.
He bears so many arms that no one can come near him, 1025
For his crossbow hangs from his padded tunic,
And I see his iron mace suspended from his saddlebow.
Unless I am helped by the One who pardoned Longinus,
He will never be defeated, for he is too well armed."
Corsolt said three words in derision: 1030
"Ah, William! What an evil heart you have.
You seem to be such a great champion,
In swordplay you are quite skilled,
But you'll never be saved by these arms!"

---

9   The "pré Noiron" (now Prati de Castello) was traditionally considered the site of St. Peter's
crucifixion as well as the garden where Nero had Christians burned. As here, it is frequently part of
an epic formula invoking "the one / the apostle we seek in Nero's Meadow," i.e., St. Peter.

Then he turned his Aragonese warhorse,   1035
Drew forth the sword that hung by his side,
And struck William such a blow
That it shattered his helm and nose guard,
Sliced through the coif of his supple hauberk,
Trimmed the hair above his forehead,   1040
And lopped off the end of his nose.
The good man was much derided for this afterwards.
The blow continued down to the saddlebow
And sliced his horse into two pieces.
It was a mighty blow, struck with such great power   1045
That three hundred links of mail hit the sand.
The sword flew from the scoundrel's hand.
Count William jumped to his feet
And drew Joyous,[10] which hung at his side;
He meant to strike Corsolt upon his helmet,   1050
But he was so huge and tall and lengthy
That he could not have reached it for all the gold in this world.
His blow struck his supple hauberk,
And three hundred links of mail hit the sand.
His old byrnie saved the Turk: 1055
He was not wounded even a little.
Corsolt said two words in derision:
"Ah, William! What an evil heart you have!
Your blows aren't worth a fig."
All the Romans cried out loudly,   1060
Including the pope, who was very frightened:
"St. Peter, my lord, help your champion!
If he dies here, the consequences will be dire:
For as long as we live, neither mass
Nor lessons will ever again be read in your church."   1065

---

10   In *The Song of Roland* (Oxford text, lines 2501, 2508, and 2989) we learn that Charlemagne's
sword is named *Joiuse* (Joyous). According to tradition, he passed this sword on to William of
Orange sometime after the defeat at Roncevaux. No text actually contains this scene, but William's
sword is *Joieuse* here and in several other epics of the William cycle.

26.

Count William with the courageous countenance
Was fully armed upon the broad mountain;
He saw that the pagan had lost his sword
After it had severed his horse's spine.
The Turk rode by farther than a crossbow's shot,   1070
Pulling out his mace as he spurred along.
He charged open-mouthed toward William,
Foaming at the mouth like an overheated beast
Chased by hounds through a thick forest.
The count saw him and raised his shield: 1075
The Turk struck it such a mighty blow
That it split and shattered from top to bottom,
Then cut the boss completely off.
A sparrowhawk in full flight
Could have passed through the hole.   1080
The mace passed near his helmet
As William ducked to avoid the encounter.
Rome would never again have been protected by him
Were it not for God and the honored Virgin.
All the Romans cried out loudly.   1085
The pope said, "What are you doing, St. Peter?
If he dies here, our future will be dire;
As long as I live and endure,
No further mass will be sung in your church."

27.

Count William was quite dazed   1090
And greatly weakened by this blow;
He was truly astonished
That the Turk was able to remain on his horse,
Having lost so much blood.
If William had wanted to, he could have unhorsed him,   1095
But he spared the horse as much as possible,
For he thought that if he could capture it,
The horse might be of great service to him.
The Saracen approached him angrily;
At the sight of William, he provoked him, saying: 1100

"Wretched Frenchman, now you are in bad shape,
For you have lost half your nose!
Now you will forever depend on Louis for your income,[11]
And your lineage will be reproached for it.
Now you see that you can do nothing to help yourself;   1105
I must return with you,
For the emir is waiting for me at his table.
He is very surprised at my long delay."
At once he leaned down toward his saddle;
He wanted to lift William fully armed   1110
Onto his horse's neck in front of him.
Seeing this, William could not believe his good luck;
He was well positioned to strike his blow,
And he struck the king—he had no wish to spare him—
Right through his gold-banded helm,   1115
So that decorations and jewels went tumbling to the ground;
And he sliced through the hood,
Ruining the fine coif
And splitting the Saracen's skull by a full hand's width.
He toppled him over onto his horse's neck;   1120
His armor was heavy; he could not pull himself back up.
"God," said William, "now I have avenged my nose;
I shall not depend on Louis for my income,
Nor will my lineage be reproached for it."
He pulled his arm from his shield-strap,   1125
And threw his shield on the battlefield with abandon;
No knight has ever been so bold!
Had the Turk been well, sound, and whole,
The battle would have resumed in great folly;
But it did not please God that he could fight any longer.   1130
Count William did not hesitate:
With his two fists he seized the steel sword
And struck the king, without sparing him,

---

11   Corsolt taunts William by predicting that he will be Louis's "prebendary"—that is, that he
will be forced to depend on Louis for food and equipment, gifts in kind that a lord bestows upon
those of his men not invested with a fief. See Frappier, *Les Chansons de geste du cycle de Guillaume
d'Orange,* 2: 87n1.

Through the straps of his banded helm;
His head and his helm went flying four feet;   1135
His body staggered, and the Saracen fell.
Count William did not wish to leave behind
The fine sword that had sliced his nose;
He tried to gird it on, but it was too long for him.
He hung it on the saddlebow of Corsolt's horse,   1139a
Then went to mount the magnificent steed,   1139b
But the stirrups were too long by a foot and a half: 1140
He shortened them a good six inches.
Count William mounted, using the stirrup;
He removed his spear,
Which he had thrust into the Saracen's body.
"God," said William, "how grateful I am to you   1145
For the horse I captured here.
I would not give it up for all the gold in Montpellier!
On this day, I greatly desired it."
He went to Rome without delay.
The pope was the first to greet him,   1150
Kissing him as soon as he had untied his helm.
How Count Bertrand, his nephew, wept,
Along with Guielin and courtly Gautier!
They had never been so afraid in their lives.
"Uncle," said Bertrand, "are you safe and sound?"   1155
—"Yes," he replied, "thank God in heaven,
Except that my nose has been shortened a bit;
I surely don't know how it could be lengthened."
The count renamed himself then and there:
"From this day forward, may all those who love and cherish me, 1160
Frenchmen and Berruiers, call me
'Short-nosed Count William the warrior.'"
From that day forward, his name could not be changed.
They rode on until they reached the main church.
The one who held William's stirrup was filled with joy.   1165
That night all rejoiced for the noble knight
Until the next morning at daybreak,
When they wished to speak of other things.
Bertrand cried, "To arms, knights!

Because my uncle won the day   1170
Against the strongest and most fearsome enemy,
We should go up against the weaker ones.
Uncle William, do take a rest,
For you have endured a horrible ordeal."
Hearing this, William laughed heartily.   1175
"Ha, Lord Bertrand, on the contrary!
Opposing me will do you no good,
For, by the apostle the pilgrims seek,
I will not fail, for all the gold in Montpellier,
To appear in the first line of combat,   1180
Where I shall wield my steel sword."
When the Romans heard him speak thus,
Even the most cowardly grew brave and nimble.
Now, let the wicked scoundrels be on their guard:
They risk delaying and waiting too long,   1185
For the Romans are going to prepare for battle!

28.
King Galafre left his tent;
He was dressed and shod like a king.
He said to his men, "Now I have lost a great deal,
Since Corsolt was struck down by such a man.   1190
The God they believe in deserves to be feared;
See to it that my tent is quickly dismantled:
Let us flee at once: what are we waiting for?
If the Romans catch sight of us,
Not a single man in our army will escape!"   1195
And they replied, "We shall heed this advice."
Twenty-five trumpets sounded all at once.
Galvanized by the alarm, the army mounted.
William heard the tumult;
He said to his men, "We have waited too long;   1200
The pagans are fleeing, those faithless scoundrels.
Now follow them, for the sake of God, King Jesus!"
The entire Roman army rode out, shouting their battle cry.
William, the noble count, stood,
Exhausted as he was, in the first line;   1205

He urged Alion on with his sharp spurs;
The horse was so wild, William could barely control it:
It seemed to the horse that its rider was quite light.
They pursued the pagans to an area between two hills.
There you would have seen an unrelenting battle,   1210
With many hands, heads, and trunks chopped off!
Count Bertrand fought vigorously.
After wielding his lance he drew his sharp sword;
Anyone he touched was split right through to the chest;
A hauberk was not worth a piece of straw;   1215
He was dealt many a blow and returned many more.
Guielin struck many blows as well,
As did Gautier of Toulouse.
But William was feared above all others.
Then King Galafre's presence was noticed;   1220
William mounted, his shield around his neck;
When Galafre saw him,   1221a
He invoked Mohammed with all his might:
"Mohammed, lord, this has gone badly for me,
Since I have not taken or captured him."
He urged on his horse with sharp spurs;   1225
Count William was not daunted in the least.
Each dealt fierce blows to the other's shiny helm;
They destroyed each other's hauberks, ripping apart the chain mail;
They felt the sharp blades piercing their sides.
God came to the aid of fearsome William,   1230
As did St. Peter, for William was his champion.
They prevented his flesh from being pierced by the king.
The noble count dealt him such a blow
That Galafre lost both his stirrups;
He fell off the horse that had borne his weight   1235
And the point of his helm penetrated the ground.
Count William stopped and stood over him;
He drew his sword with its sharp blade:
He was about to chop off his head above the trunk,
When God performed a powerful miracle,   1240
For many a sorrowful and angry captive
Was released from prison on that day.

29.

Count William was truly a fine knight:
Before him he saw the king completely toppled over.
Had he wanted, he could have chopped off his head,   1245
But then the king cried out to him for mercy and pity.
"Valiant knight, do not kill me, for you are William,
But rather take me alive; you could gain much from it.
I will return the powerful King Gaifier to you,
Along with his daughter and his noble wife   1250
And thirty thousand wretched captives,
Who will lose their heads if I die."
—"By St. Denis," said the proud-faced count,
"This is reason enough to spare you."
Count William stood firm in his stirrups;   1255
The king offered him his fine steel sword.
William sent him to the pope as a prisoner,
Along with three hundred other prisoners.
William then said to the king, "Have them untied."
And Galafre replied, "You are speaking foolishly,   1260
For, by the cross sought by pilgrims,
You will not have anything worth even a penny
Until I am baptized over the fonts,
For Mohammed can help me no longer!"
—"God," said William, "may you be praised!"   1265
The pope did not delay,
But had a baptismal font prepared immediately;
They baptized the king over the fonts.
William the warrior served as his godfather,
Along with Guielin and the courteous Gautier,   1270
And thirty other valiant knights,
All of whom were distinguished noblemen.
But they did not change the king's name;[12]
Instead, they established his name as a Christian one.
They ordered water and sat down for a meal;   1275
When they had had enough to sustain them,

---

12   Converted Saracens are often given a new name at baptism. In *The Conquest of Orange*, for
example, William's beloved queen Orable takes the name Guibourc.

Count William leapt to his feet:
"Ah, noble king, for the sake of righteous God,
Noble godson, come forward:
How will our prisoners be returned to us,   1280
Those who are bound and confined in your ships?"
The king replied, "I will have to think it over,
Because if the Saracens and pagans knew
That I had been baptized over the fonts,
They would rather see me flayed alive   1285
Than return to me anything worth even a penny.
But now let me be stripped of my clothing
And put upon a pitiful packhorse,
Close enough that I can shout to them.
Have all your men ready   1290
Beneath this grove of olive trees;
If the Saracens make an effort
To help and rescue me,
Let all of you be prepared with your lances lowered."
—"God," said William, "by your holy pity,   1295
Never has there been a better convert!"
They acceded to all of his wishes,
Except to be beaten: they spared him that much.
Instead, they covered him with the blood of a hare.
They did not pause until reaching the Tiber.   1300
King Galafre began to shout;
He cried out loudly, "Champion, lord nephew,
Son of a baron, come help me!
By Mohammed, I badly need it.
The God they serve should be greatly esteemed.   1305
A crowned king should not be shackled;
But I will be spared if you agree to an exchange:
Have their wretched prisoners returned to them."
Champion replied, "Now Mohammed has come to your aid,
Since you will be spared by means of an exchange."   1310
They had the ship pulled in to shore.
They dragged out the wretched prisoners;
But they had been so badly beaten and abused,
Since the Saracens had defeated and chased them down,

That every prisoner was covered with blood on his stomach,   1315
Shoulders, body, and head.
William the warrior wept with pity.

30.
When the prisoners were released from the ships,
Every single one was covered with blood on his face,
Shoulders, and entire torso.   1320
William Fierebrace wept with pity.
Seeing the pope, he pulled him aside:
"My lord," he said, "in the name of God, the heavenly one,
Many of these gentlemen are bare-chested;
Let us give them furs and cloaks and mantles;   1325
Let them all be given gold and silver,
So that they may return to their lands."
The pope replied, "Noble, honorable man,
Everyone should be generous in honoring others;
It is right and just to follow this advice."   1330
They went to Rome without delay;
They unpacked their trunks for the prisoners,
And gave them clothing, furs, and mantles.
All those present received silver and gold,
Enabling them to return to their lands.   1335

31.
When the Christians had returned to Rome,
Count William sat down beside a thicket.
Now behold the powerful King Gaifier,
Who fell immediately at William's feet, saying:
"Noble lord, you came to my aid;   1340
You rescued me from the hands of the evil enemy,
Who would have led me in chains into their land;
I would never again have seen my domains or my fiefs.
I have a daughter; there is none so beautiful under the heavens.
I offer her to you gladly and willingly;   1345
If you wish to accept and take her as your wife,
You will receive half of my land,
And after my death you will be my heir."

The count replied, "I must seek advice on the matter."
Seeing the pope, he drew him aside: 1350
"My lord," he said, "should I marry this woman?"
—"Yes, fair lord, gladly and willingly.
You are a young knight[13] in need of a fief."
The count replied, "Then I must agree."
They brought the young woman before him: 1355
No man of flesh, no pilgrim or palmer,
As far as he might ride or roam,
Could meet a more beautiful lady.
William the warrior would have married her,
But an unexpected situation prevented him from doing so,   1360
As you will hear before sunset.

32.
Would you like to hear of her beauty?
No man of flesh, no matter where he traveled,
Would be able to find a more beautiful lady.
Short-nosed William would have married her,   1365
But an unexpected difficulty stopped him from doing so,
As you will hear before nightfall.
Two messengers arrived suddenly in haste
From France; they had pushed their steeds so hard
That they had exhausted and worn them out.   1370
They sought William and asked for him so much
That they found the count in the church
Where he was about to marry his beloved,
And the noble and valiant pope
Had donned his vestments and was ready to sing mass.   1375
William had taken the ring to marry the lady
When the messengers threw themselves at his feet:
"Have mercy, William, in the name of Christian charity,
You have paid little attention to Louis,
For the noble and valiant Charlemagne has died,   1380

---

13   The pope uses the word *bachelers*, which can designate a young man of any social class, but
most often a knight. The emphasis is on the *bacheler*'s youth and, in this passage, his status as an
unmarried man without a fief. See Jean Flori, "Qu'est-ce qu'un *bacheler*?"

And Louis has a great inheritance.
Traitors want to dispossess him of it
And crown another king,
The son of Richard of the city of Rouen.
They will shame the whole country,   1385
Most noble lord, if you do not save Louis."
Hearing this, William bowed his head;
He saw the pope and turned to speak to him:
"Lord," he said, "what counsel do you give me?"
The pope said, "God be praised!   1390
One should give counsel to the one who seeks it:
As penance, I direct you
To rescue your lord, Louis.
It will be a great shame if he is disinherited."
The count responded, "As you wish,   1395
Your counsel will never be refused."
William kissed the fair-faced lady
And she kissed him and did not stop crying.
They were separated in this fashion
And never saw each other again.   1400
"Lord William," said the valiant pope,
"You should return to sweet France;
Emir Galafre will stay here
To guard Rome in your name."
The count responded, "You speak folly.   1405
I have never been accused of treason:
I shall always guard against it."
—"Lord William," said the valiant pope,
"You should go to sweet France
And take a thousand knights with you   1410
And thirty beasts of burden loaded with gold and silver.
You should take what you have conquered."
The count responded, "I thank you for that."

33.
One Sunday, two weeks after Easter,
William Fierebrace was in Rome;   1415
He was about to take a wife and marry—

He had quickly forgotten Orable!—[14]
When two messengers from France arrived
Who brought him heartbreaking news,
That the emperor Charlemagne was dead.   1420
Louis had inherited the borderlands;
But traitors—may God bring them ill—
Wanted to make the son of bearded Richard of Rouen
King of France in front of the barons.
William Fierebrace wept out of compassion.   1425
He begged leave of the wise pope,
Who gave him four thousand armed men
And thirty mules packed with gold and silver.
At the moment of his departure all the barons wept.
The count left without delay,   1430
He crossed the Saint Bernard Pass, which was difficult.
I do not know how much of their journey to tell you;
They did not stop or tarry until Brie.

34.
Short-Nosed William the marquis took his leave.
I cannot tell you of his entire journey;   1435
He traveled straight to Brie.
He encountered a pilgrim on his path
With a scarf around his neck and a staff of ash in his hand.
You've never seen such a lively pilgrim!
He had a beard as white as a flower in April.   1440
When William saw him, he spoke to him,
"Where are you from, brother?"—"From Tours, the town of St.
    Martin."
—"Do you have any news to tell us?"
—"Yes, my lord, about little Louis:
Charlemagne is dead, the king of Saint-Denis,   1445
And the country has passed to Louis.

---

14   The character Orable does not appear until the last story in this trilogy, *The Conquest of Orange*. The mention of her name here in *The Coronation of Louis*, before she actually appears chronologically in the action of the trilogy, is a later interpolation in the manuscripts based on her appearance in another text, the *Enfances Guillaume*. See Frappier, *Les Chansons de geste du cycle de Guillaume d'Orange*, 2: 91n1.

Traitors—may God curse them—
Want to make white-bearded
Richard of Rouen the king of France.
But a noble abbot—may God bless him—   1450
Has taken refuge with the child
In a crypt of the monastery of St. Martin,
Where they expect to be killed.
Alas! May God help them!" continued the noble pilgrim,
"Where are the valiant knights   1455
And the lineage of the brave Count Aymeri?
They were accustomed to supporting their lord.
By the cross where the body of our Lord was placed,
If I had the power to help him,
I would harm the traitors so badly   1460
That they would abandon the idea of betraying their lord!"
Hearing this, William burst out laughing;
He addressed Bertrand:
"Have you ever heard such a courtly pilgrim?
If he had been able to help Louis,   1465
They never would have conceived such a wicked plan."
They gave the pilgrim ten ounces of gold
And he left very happy.
William left and took up his route again.
Happy is the one who has many friends.   1470
William looked ahead of him in the path
And saw a hundred forty knights approaching,
With bright weapons and mounted on prized steeds.
The marquis Gauldin the Brown was leading them,
And with him was the brave Savaris.   1475
They were nephews of proud-faced William;
They were going to France to rescue Louis.
They were pleasantly surprised to cross paths,
And they embraced because they were nephews and friends.
The abbot of noble lineage who was keeping young Louis 1480
Did not anticipate their arrival.
If he could protect and preserve Louis a while longer
And keep him from the lineage of Alori,
Help would arrive by the third day.

35.

William the noble warrior left,   1485
Accompanied by twelve hundred knights.
He made an announcement to his company;
Each one rode up, whether on a steed or a warhorse,
And he said to them without delay
That they should not spare their horses,   1490
For if anyone lost his packhorse, he would give him a warhorse.
"I want to be there at the beginning of this evil plan.
I want to know as soon as possible
Who wants to be king of France and rule the country.
But by the apostle whom palmers venerate,   1495
He seems now to be so proud and haughty,
That I shall place such a crown on his head
As will make his brains spill out all the way down to his feet!"
The Romans said, "This is a brave-hearted man.
May God bring grief to the one who fails him!"   1500
I do not know what I should tell you about their journey;
It did not take them long to get from there to Tours.
William wanted to act wisely.
He placed a thousand knights in four positions of ambush
And took with him two hundred well-armed knights,   1505
Who wore shiny lined hauberks;
They wore bright laced helms over their coifs of mail,
And they girded on their polished steel blades.
The squires remained close to them
With their knights' strong shields and sharp spears,   1510
Which they could provide if needed.
It did not take them long to reach the gates,
Where they found the gatekeeper, to whom they called out:
"Open the gate, don't make us wait!
We've come to help Duke Richard,   1515
Whose son will be crowned today in the church
As the Franks have decided."
Hearing this, the gatekeeper became enraged.
He invoked God, the righteous Father:
"By Holy Mary," said the gatekeeper,   1520
"Louis, my lord, you're helpless!

If he who judges all does not intervene,
You will not leave here without being torn to pieces.
Alas! May God help you!" said the gallant gatekeeper,
"Where are the valiant knights   1525
And the descendants of Aymeri the warrior
Who always helped their rightful lord?"
He said to William, "You will not set foot in here.
There are already too many scoundrels inside,
And I don't wish you to increase their numbers.   1530
It is a wonder that the earth supports you.
May it please the Lord of heaven
To make it crumble under your feet
And restore Louis to his land.
The world would be avenged of evil people."   1535
Hearing this, William was joyful and happy.
He called to Bertrand, "Listen, my lord nephew,
Have you ever heard a gatekeeper speak so well?
If we reveal our hearts to him
He may serve us well today."   1540

36.
"Friend, fair brother," said valiant William,
"Foolishly you have kept me from entering your gatehouse,
But if you knew in which land I was born
And who my people and family are,
Based on what I just heard you say,   1545
You would willingly and happily open it."
Hearing this, the gatekeeper jumped to his feet   1546a
And said, "May God be praised!"
He opened the window so that he could see William:
"Noble lord, if I dared to speak,
I would ask in what land you were born   1550
And who your people and your family are."
—"Certainly," said William, "you will now hear the truth,
For out of fear of no man have I ever hidden my name.
I am William, I was born in Narbonne."
The gatekeeper said, "May God be praised!   1555
Lord William, I know what you seek,

Your lineage has never been cowardly.
The evil Richard has entered here
With seven hundred armed knights.
Noble lord, you have few men   1560
To fight against their great numbers."
William responded, "We will have plenty!
At four ambush positions outside are stationed
A thousand knights, armed and ready for combat,
And I have two hundred armed with me,   1565
Who are wearing their shiny hauberks under their capes
And green-gold jeweled helms over their coifs of mail.
Many squires follow close behind them
To whom we can turn at need."
The gatekeeper said, "May God be praised!   1570
If one were to ask my advice,
All the ambush positions would be abandoned
And the knights sent for discreetly.
The traitors are concentrated together inside.
Where will you look for them when you have already found
     them?   1575
On this day, if the truth be known,
Before the break of dawn
You will be able to do with them as you wish.
A man who wishes to accomplish such a task
Must be more ferocious than a wild boar in the forest!"   1580
Hearing this, William lowered his head
And called to Bertrand, "Dear nephew, listen,
Have you ever heard a gatekeeper speak so well?"

37.
When the gatekeeper heard the news
Of valiant William who exuded prowess,   1585
He turned his head toward the palace,
Took a glove, held it in his right hand,
Then cried out in a loud and beautiful voice:
"I defy you, Richard, you and your lands,
And I do not wish to be in your service any longer!   1590
Since you have sought to commit treason,

It is only right that you should perish."
The gatekeeper opened the gate for William;
He unlocked and opened it at once.
William and his handsome entourage entered,   1595
And the gatekeeper spoke softly to him:
"Noble knight, go now and take your vengeance
On the traitors who have shown themselves against you."
Hearing this, William lowered his head
And quickly called a squire: 1600
"Go to Lord Gautier of Tudela on my behalf,
And also share the news with Gontier of Rome,
That whoever wishes to spoil and conquer,
Should come join me discreetly,
For the gate has been opened to me."   1605
And the squire left without wasting time.
Those lying in ambush quickly rushed forward
And entered the gates that were opened for them.
When Richard's men saw them from the windows and the walls,
They thought they were the men they had sent for,   1610
But they will receive other news this day
That will be both painful and terrible for them.

38.
Count William called to the gatekeeper:
"Friend, fair brother, please advise me:
I have many people whom I need to lodge."   1615
—"In God's name, my lord, I do not know how to advise you.
There is not a vault, crypt, or upper room
That is not full of arms and horses,
And the knights are hunkered down in the houses.
You have the power to change things: 1620
Have them surrender their armor and have it seized,
Anyone who does not wish to give it up willingly
Must offer his head to be cut off!"
William answered, "You have advised me well,
In the name of St. Denis, and I ask nothing further of you.   1625
You will no longer be guardian or gatekeeper;
You will now be my principal advisor."

He called to Bertrand, "Listen, lord nephew,
Have you ever heard a gatekeeper speak so well?
Arm him as a knight." 1630
Bertrand answered, "Gladly, my lord."
He looked him over from head to toe
And noticed that he was noble, handsome, and well built;
He armed him as one does a knight:
With a strong hauberk and a steel helm, 1635
A good sword and a sharp spear,
A steed, a workhorse, a squire,
A palfrey, a mule, and a packhorse.
He was well rewarded for his service.
Count William called to Gautier 1640
The Toulousain—or so I've heard him called—
The son of his sister, a noble knight:
"Son of a noble woman, go in my name
To the gate leading to Poitiers,
Along with twenty knights. 1645
And make sure no one under heaven,
Neither cleric nor priest, no matter how well he prays,
Leaves without being killed and cut to pieces."
And Gautier answered, "Gladly, fair lord."

39.
Count William, the short-nosed marquis, 1650
Called out to Floire of Plessis:
"To the gate facing Paris
You will go for me, brave and prized knight,
And with you up to twenty knights.
Make sure no one born of a mother 1655
Leaves without being killed and cut to pieces."
And Floire responded, "Exactly as you wish."
There was not a rampart or gate or postern
Where the count did not have his knights.
He went straight to the church without hindrance. 1660
He dismounted onto the paved street,
Entered the church, and made the sign of the cross on his forehead.
On the marble, in front of the crucifix,

William the marquis knelt
And prayed to God who was hanged on the cross   1665
That he send him his lord Louis.
At that moment a cleric, Gautier, came up to him.
He easily recognized William the marquis
And put his finger on his shoulder
Hard enough so that William felt it.   1670
The count arose and showed him his face:
"What do you want, brother? Be careful not to lie."
He responded, "I shall soon tell you,
Since you came to rescue Louis:
Close the doors of the church of St. Martin.   1675
There are eighty clerics and canons inside,
And highly esteemed bishops and abbots
Who devised this evil plan for money.
Louis will be disinherited today
If you and God do not protect him.   1680
Cut off their heads! In God's name, I implore you!
I take responsibility for any sin committed in the church,
For they are all traitors and cowards, and they have failed."
Hearing this, William burst out laughing:
"Blessed be the hour that such a cleric was raised!   1685
Where shall I find my lord Louis?"
—"In God's name," the cleric answered,
"I shall take you to him if God wills it and I live."
He did not waste any time going to the monastery:
He went straightaway to the large crypt   1690
Where he found his lord Louis.
The noble cleric took him by the hand:
"Son of a worthy king, do not be dismayed,
So help me God, because you have more friends
Than you had this morning at daybreak.   1695
William the marquis has just arrived
With twelve hundred worthy knights
To look for you in this church.
There is no rampart, gate, or postern
Where he has not placed his knights."   1700
Hearing this, Louis rejoiced

And lost no time going to the church.
The noble abbot spoke to him:
"Son of a worthy king, do not be afraid.
Here is William who has pledged you his faith;   1705
Fall at his feet and ask for mercy."
The child answered, "Just as you wish."

40.
The noble abbot spoke first to Louis:
"Son of a worthy king, do not worry,
Here is William, fall at his feet."   1710
The youth responded, "Gladly, my lord."
He knelt before the count
And immediately kissed his feet
And the shoes the count was wearing.
William the warrior did not recognize him,   1715
Because there was little light in the church:
"Get up, child," said the worthy count,
"No man created by God has wronged me so much
That if he were to fall at my feet
I would not willingly and gladly pardon him."   1720
And the abbot spoke on Louis's behalf:
"In God's name, I do not wish to conceal it from you,
This is Louis, the son of proud-faced Charlemagne.
He will be killed and torn to pieces today
If God and you do not come to his aid."   1725
Hearing this, William ran to embrace him
And immediately grabbed him by the waist and lifted him up:
"In God's name, child, you fooled me!
Who told you to fall at my feet?
Of all men, it is I who should come to your aid."   1730
Then he called out to his noble knights:
"I ask that you render a judgment for me:
When a man is tonsured in a church
And is supposed to live to read his psalter,
Should he then commit treason for money?"   1735
—"Not at all, my lord," said the knights.
—"And should he do it, what would be the penalty?"

—"He should be hanged as a common thief."
William responded, "You have advised me well,
By St. Denis, and I ask for nothing more."   1740

41.
With stout heart, Count William
Heard the judgment of his barons.
He went up to the chancel in haste,
Where he found the bishops, abbots,
And clerics who had betrayed their lord.   1745
He grabbed all the crosses from their hands   1745a
And delivered them to Louis, his rightful lord.
The noble count took him by the sides and embraced him,
Kissing him four times on his cheeks.
Count William wasted no time;
He hastened up to the chancel,   1750
Where he had left the bishops and abbots.
To avoid sinning in the church, he did not touch his weapons;
Instead, his barons beat them with staffs and scattered them.
They chased and dragged them from the church,
Then commended them to eighty devils.   1755
He who wishes to betray his lord
Deserves to pay the price!

42.
Count William was very chivalrous.
He called out to Louis, his lord:
"My lord," he said, "hear me out: 1760
I would like us to send a messenger
To tell Acelin, on your behalf,
That he should come and make amends with Louis, his lord."
Louis said, "My lord, I approve."
William called out to Aleaume the baron: 1765
"Go tell that arrogant Acelin for me
That he must come to make amends to his rightful lord, Louis,
Right away, for he lodges a complaint against him."
Aleaume responded, "Shall I go alone?"
—"Yes, fair brother, and take a staff in your hand."   1770

—"And if he asks how many strong we are?"
—"Tell him we have forty companions,
And if he refuses to come,
Tell him in front of his companions
That he will be so shamed before nightfall   1775
That he would not want to be there for all the riches in Mâcon!"
Aleaume answered, "We shall do you as you desire,
By that apostle they seek in Nero's Meadow;
We have nothing to lose with this message."
He mounted on a mule from Aragon   1780
And went through the streets spurring on his mule.
He did not stop until he reached Acelin's lodging,
Where he found him and many of his companions.
He called out loudly to him in front of everyone:
"Lord Acelin, noble and courteous man,   1785
You are being summoned by William the noble man,
The strong-armed, the lion-hearted.
Come to make amends to your rightful lord, Louis,
Right away, for he complains much about you."
Hearing this, Acelin lowered his chin: 1790
"Friend," he said, "I understand what you're saying.
Tell me how many companions your uncle has."
—"In God's name, my lord, he has thirty knights."
Acelin said, "May God be praised!
Go and tell noble William for me   1795
That he should do as the others have.
The crown should be given to me:
France will be lost with this boy,
He isn't worth a button!
Count William is a wonderfully brave man,   1800
But he has no land or fief.
I shall give him all at his discretion;
He will have land as he wishes,
Ten mules loaded with pure gold and gold pieces;
Then he will be a wonderfully rich man."   1805
—"Indeed," said Aleaume, "you speak empty words!
He can't be bought for all of Avalon's gold.
He still summons you, why should we keep it from you?

We have not yet told you everything:
If you firmly refuse this request,   1810
You will be so shamed this very day before nightfall
That you would not want this for all the world's riches!"
Acelin said, "May God be praised!
Since I can find no peace nor love with him,
I defy him! Tell him so on our behalf."   1815
Aleaume answered, "We have heard you clearly.
I also say to you, on our behalf:
I defy you, and this in front of your barons!"

43.
Acelin was very haughty and proud.
He looked Aleaume over from head to toe   1820
And noticed that he was noble, handsome, and strong.
He could tell he was a squire:
"Friend, fair brother, you are poorly instructed,
You who shame me in front of my knights.
As for your uncle, I wouldn't give a penny for him.   1825
Since I find neither peace nor love with him,
I defy him and shall cut off his head
And tear him to pieces today!
I have with me seven hundred knights
And four very worthy counts   1830
Who are willing to lose limbs for me.
In fact, if you weren't the messenger,
I'd have you beheaded
And torn limb from limb."
Aleaume answered, "Cursed be the one who fears you!"   1835
He left the court without even taking leave.
Acelin prepared his men.
Noble Aleaume mounted his horse
And rode through the streets without delay.
He encountered William first,   1840
Who asked him, "How did you fare?"
—"In God's name, my lord, there is no love with Acelin
And he does not acknowledge Louis as his lord.
When I told him the names of knights,

You were immediately threatened,   1845
And he said he'd cut off your head;
And if I had not been the messenger,
He would have torn me limb from limb,
Burned me alive, or had me drowned."
Hearing this, William thought he would lose his mind.   1850
His companions searched and ransacked all the lodgings
And made a pile of all the weapons;
Whoever did not wish to give up his weapons willingly
Risked nothing less than having his head cut off.
The bourgeois were fleeing,   1855
But Count William had them stopped and bound.
May God heap shame upon the traitors
Who instigated the evil plot
And who tried to flee on their horses!
They sped toward the gates without stopping,   1860
But at each one they found an unwelcoming gatekeeper.
They had to leave bribes there,
For they wished to avoid prison,
And no one could have persuaded them otherwise.
Count William began to spur ahead   1865
To the lodging of the noble bourgeois Hungier.
He found Acelin there seated on a step,
But he was so arrogant and proud
That he did not even deign to stand.
Seeing this, William thought he would lose his mind.   1870
Since he was alone and Acelin had many men,   1870a
He sounded his horn sharply.
If you had only seen the knights waiting in ambush come forward!
Behold Bertrand and Gautier
And with them a host of valiant knights!
There you would have seen a terrible battle begin,   1875
Many lances broken, many shields pierced,
And many hauberks torn to pieces, their chain mail unfastened!
When the traitors saw this terrible battle begin,
And William's men fight so fiercely,   1878a
The infamous deceivers were sorely afraid
As they realized their struggle was useless.   1880

They threw down their blades at the feet of their enemy
And pleaded mercy with their hands clasped together.
The count had them held and bound.
Acelin fled immediately;
Count William followed closely behind   1885
And reprimanded him most harshly:
"Lord Acelin, turn around
And come to be crowned in the church.
We shall put such a crown on your head
That your brains will spill down to your feet!"   1890

44.
Count William was a proud person;
He saw Acelin and spoke to him sternly:
"Filthy traitor, may God destroy you!
Why have you dishonored your rightful lord?
Richard, your father, never wore a crown."   1895
Behold Bertrand, who had a long sword;
When he saw him, William spoke firmly:
"Fair nephew Bertrand, we ask for your advice
On how we shall lay waste to this land,
And how we shall destroy this traitor."   1900
And Bertrand said, "What do you think, my fair uncle?
Let's push a crown onto his head so far
That his brains spill out of his mouth!"
He came forth bearing his long sword
And was going to strike him in front of a hundred men   1905
When Lord William, his uncle, cried out:
"Fair nephew," he said, "Don't touch him!
May it not please God, who created the entire world,
That he die by the sword of a worthy man.
I shall instead kill him in a shameful way,   1910
So that all his heirs will be greatly humiliated."

45.
Count William was a courageous knight.
He approached the haughty one in a ferocious manner,
Like a leopard about to devour someone,

But did not want to touch him with the weapon he held. 1915
He saw a sharp stake in a trellis;
As he passed by he seized it,
Struck Acelin on the forehead,
And spilled his blood and brains down to his feet.
He struck him dead on the spot. 1920
"Monjoie!" he cried, "As St. Denis is my witness,
Louis is avenged of this king!"
Count William began to spur ahead
And rode straight to the main church,
Where he came before Louis, his rightful lord, 1925
And ran up and embraced him tightly:
"Young lord, who else do you have to worry about?
I have avenged you on Richard's son. 1927a
He will never again go to wage war,
No matter who might beg him to do so."
—"God," said the child, "I thank you! 1930
If I were now avenged of his father,
I would be very happy and joyful."
—"God," said William, "who can tell me where he is?"
Someone told him Richard was in the church.
The count went there immediately, 1935
Followed by eighty knights.
He found Richard leaning on the altar,
Ignored the fact that he was in a church,
Seized him by the hair,
And doubled him over. 1940
Then William raised his right fist, struck him on the neck,
And knocked him down all dazed at his feet.
One could have dismembered him
And he would not have moved a hand or foot.
Seeing this, William began to cry out to him: 1945
"Get out of here, scoundrel! May God destroy you!"
He asked for scissors, tonsured his head,
And stretched him out on the marble;
Then he cried out to him in front of the knights:
"This is how one should punish a traitor 1950
Who sought to betray and deceive his rightful lord!"

The counts and the dukes pleaded so much
That they restored peace between the count and William.
Richard first pardoned William for the death of his son.
Peace was made between them before they left the church,   1955
And they kissed one another in front of a hundred knights.
But this agreement was not worth a penny,
Because Richard and his men soon sought to kill and maim William
In the woods with a steel knife.
But God would not allow or grant it.   1960
Count William wanted to waste no time
And called out to the good abbot Gautier:
"I am going to the land of Poitiers,
For many traitors are living there;
But if it please God, I shall hunt them down.   1965
I do not wish to leave my rightful lord alone.
Look after him well, and if he should want any entertainment,
Let him take with him at least a hundred knights;
For by the apostle that the palmers invoke,
If I receive word upon my return   1970
That Louis has suffered harm,   1970a
All your orders will not prevent you
From having your heads cut off
And your bodies destroyed and mutilated."
—"I swear by my head," said the abbot, "he will be protected
Better than the relics in the church."   1975
Count William was a good knight;
He sent letters throughout the land
To convene the brave knights.
Before two weeks had passed,
He had assembled more than thirty thousand.   1980
Then they set out together for Poitiers.
Three entire years passed   1981a
During which there was not a day, no matter how grand or
    important,
When William did not have his green-gold helm laced,
His sword attached to his side, or was armed on his horse.
There was never a feast day when one prays,   1985
Not even Christmas which one is obliged to observe,

When he was not armed on his horse.
The knight suffered great hardship
To help and uphold his lord.

46.
William the brave was three full years   1990
In Poitou to conquer the land;
And there was not a day, no matter how important,
Neither Easter, nor Christmas,
Nor All Saints' Day which one is obliged to observe,
When he was not wearing his burnished helm,   1995
Armed on his steed, with his sword hanging at his side.
The young man suffered great hardship
To protect and defend his lord.

47.
Proud Count William
Went to Bordeaux on the Gironde,   2000
Where he conquered the powerful king Amaronde,
Who received his crown in Louis's name
Along with vast and large fiefs.

48.
Count William was very courageous.
He went next to Pierrelarge,   2005
Where he conquered Dagobert of Carthage
Who held his territory from wise Louis,
Along with his vast and large fiefs.

49.
Valiant Count William
Headed to Amadore;   2010
He besieged Saint-Gilles one morning
And took the town very quickly.
He did something that pleased Jesus:
He kept the church from being destroyed.
He took Julien, who guarded the land,   2015
And who gave William as many hostages as he wished

In order to guarantee the peace.
William said something that pleased many of his men:
"Pack up your armor, noble men of honor,
Each of you will return to his land,   2020
To the woman he married."

50.
Short-nosed Count William the warrior
Rode toward sweet France,
But he left knights in Poitou,
In the fortresses and mighty castles.   2025
He took with him two hundred well-armed knights
And began to approach Brittany
Until he reached Mont-Saint-Michel.
He stayed there two days, then left on the third.
He took up his journey again by way of the Cotentin Peninsula. 2030
I do not have much to tell you about his travels.
The duke wasted no time in going to Rouen
Where he stayed in the main part of the town.
But he did one thing I consider to be reckless:
He did not hesitate to pass or ride   2035
Through the land of the old duke, Richard,
Whose son he had killed with a large stake,
Because the noble knight had confidence
That they had reconciled and made peace.
But this agreement was not worth a penny,   2040
For Richard and his men wanted to murder and mutilate him.
"Indeed," said Richard, "I should be enraged
To see, riding through my domain, the man
Who took from me the best heir
There ever was for ruling a land.   2045
But by the apostle whom the palmers venerate,
He will be punished before he leaves."
—"In God's name," said his knights,
"We shall not touch him in this land,
Because the inhabitants will come to his aid   2050
And it is not good to commit treason."
And Richard responded, "I am very angry!

I shall let the duke know, in a friendly manner,
That I wish to ride with him to sweet France.
There will be sixteen of us well armed.   2055
If we can get him away from his men,
Each of us will have a good steel knife
And he will be murdered and mutilated."
Fifteen knights pledged their assistance,
But it would have been better for them if they had left him,   2060
Because they were going to be shamed and disgraced.
My God! What a shame the proud-faced count was totally unaware!
In the morning he mounted his horse and decided to ride
To Lyons-la-Forêt, a vast forest.
William and his knights dismounted in a moor   2065
And peasants brought them something to eat.
After the brave knights had eaten,
They took a nap under the trees.
Seeing this, William had great pity for them.
He called for his weapons to arm himself,   2070
And they brought them to him right away.
He put on his hauberk, laced his banded helm,
And hung at his side his sword with a gold-carved handle.
They brought to him his horse, Alion.
The count mounted with his left stirrup,   2075
Hung a quartered shield around his neck,
And took in his hand a sharp spear
To which his gonfalon was attached by fifteen nails.
He took with him only two knights;
They went to the river to relax,   2080
But behold old Duke Richard
Who had been spying on him all day
With his fifteen courageous knights!
Seeing this, William was very troubled.

51.
Count William rode to a hill.   2085
Behold Duke Richard the Red
And with him fifteen hardy horsemen!
Seeing this, William was very anxious;

He called to both his companions
And spoke in a very low voice to them: 2090
"Barons," he said, "tell me what we shall do.
Richard the Red is coming toward us,
And he hates me more than anyone in the world:
Everyone knows well that I killed his son.
But we were nonetheless reconciled;   2095
Peace was made in the church at Tours."
And they answered, "Why are you afraid of him?
Rather, spur ahead and ride up to the bridge
And greet him politely and in a friendly manner.
If he doesn't accept your greeting,   2100
Hold up your shield decorated with a lion,
And we shall not fail you for all the gold in this world!"
William answered, "Thank you, my barons."

52.
Count William arrived at the bridge first,
Where he saw the duke and began to speak to him: 2105
"Duke," William said, "may God protect you!
Do I have any reason to be wary of you?
We made peace between us,
In the church at Tours.
It was there that we kissed in the presence of a hundred knights." 2110
—"Indeed," said Richard, "you know how to make up a story!
You took away from me the greatest heir
There ever was under heaven.
But by the apostle whom the palmers venerate,
You will be so battered before you leave here,   2115
That neither God nor man will be able to help you
Or prevent me from cutting off your head
And ripping all the limbs off your body!"
—"Foul wretch," said the count, "may God destroy you!
I don't value you any more than a rabid dog!"   2120
He spurred Alion with his golden spurs,
Struck Richard on his quartered shield,
And broke it and pierced through under the central buckle.
He smashed his shiny hauberk to pieces

And pushed his steel blade into his left side,   2125
So that blood gushed from both sides of it.
Richard's good steed threw its rider
And the point of his helm stuck in the ground
With such force that two of the laces came undone.
William stopped over him and drew his steel blade;   2130
I think he would have cut off his head,
But behold the fifteen knights who arrived, may God destroy them,
And who attacked William the warrior!
Whoever had seen the count assault all of them
And strike them down with heavy blows from his polished blade   2135
Would have had much pity for this noble man.
His companions came to help him,
And each one cut down his opponent.
The Father of justice came to their aid so well
That they killed and dismembered ten of them.   2140
The five others fled, wounded;
Count William followed them on horseback
And hurled villainous insults at them.

53.
The five fled up to the top of a knoll.
Count William chased closely behind;   2145
He taunted them sharply:
"Lord barons, for God the heavenly King,
How will this great shame be tolerated?
We shall take prisoner your rightful lord.
By God, you will be hard pressed to take him back!"   2150
And they answered, "In God's name, have mercy, William!
Noble knight, you should be king
Or head of a great, rich land.
May God help us! You can easily defeat us,
For our bowels are hanging out over our saddles!   2155
The soundest among us cannot even walk."
Hearing this, William turned around.

54.
When William heard them plead for mercy,

He would not have touched one of them even if he were torn limb
    from limb.
He quickly turned around. 2160
They took all the weapons from the ten dead knights
And took and bound Duke Richard.
Just like a coffer on a mule,
They led him on a rapid steed.
They did not delay in reaching the rest of their troops. 2165
When they arrived, they found their companions awake.
"Uncle William," said Bertrand the warrior,
"I see blood on your steel blade
And your shield is damaged.
You must have started some sort of bad affair, 2170
Because you seem troubled and distressed to me."
—"Indeed," said William, "noble lord nephew,
When I left here to ride around, 2172a
I took with me only two knights.
I ran across old Duke Richard,
Who had been spying on me all day, 2175
He and fifteen other hardy knights.
He began to reproach me for the death of his son
And wanted to chop off all my limbs.
The righteous Father came to our aid so well
That we killed and dismembered ten, 2180
And five fled hurt and wounded.
Behold their weapons and horses.
We bound and brought with us Duke Richard."
And Bertrand said, "God be praised!"

55.
"Uncle William," said valiant Bertrand, 2185
"You act as though you don't want to live anymore."
—"Nephew," said William, "I beg your pardon,
I would have gladly spent all my youth in pain
So that this king would have his inheritance."
Then they prepared themselves to continue their journey. 2190
They pushed on and rode so hard
That they arrived at the city of Orléans.

There William found King Louis
And delivered Richard to him as a prisoner.
Louis had him thrown into his prison, 2195
And he was there so long, as I have heard tell,
That he died of grief and fatigue.
Then William thought he could rest,
Hunt in the forests and along the river;
But this would never happen as long as he lived. 2200
Behold two messengers who arrived in such great haste
From Rome that they had worn out their steeds;
They themselves were exhausted, destroyed, and defeated.
They sought and asked repeatedly for the king
Until they found William and Louis. 2205
The messengers fell at their feet and cried for mercy:
"Have mercy, noble count, in the name of the God of majesty!
You seem to have forgotten the young woman
To whom you pledged yourself.
The valiant Gaifier of Spoleto has died, 2210
And counts, dukes, and peers are seeking her hand,
But she wants to give her love only to you.
I have more bad news:
The rich emir, Galafre, has died,
The one you led to the font and had baptized. 2215
The pope, as well, has met his end.
Guy the German has assembled his army
And taken the main fortifications of Rome.
The whole country will suffer,
Noble lord, if you don't save it!" 2220
Hearing this, William bowed his head toward the ground,
And Louis began to cry.
Seeing this, William thought he would lose his mind:
"Ha! You poor, weak and foolish king!
I thought I was prepared to defend and maintain you 2225
Against everyone in Christendom.
But now all the world despises you,
And I have to use up my youth in your service,
Until you have all that you want.
Summon your men and barons 2230

And may all the young men come too,
Whose steeds and warhorses are lame and unshod,
Whose armor is torn and shredded;
All those who serve in poor seigneuries.
Let them come to me, and I shall give them plenty   2235
Of gold, silver, minted coins,
Spanish warhorses, and well-maintained mules,
Which I have brought here from the city of Rome.
In Spain I also conquered so much
That I don't know where to put a tenth of it.   2240
Never will a noble man find that I'm cheap,
For I shall give him all that he needs and more."
The king answered, "May God bless you!"
They had their documents and letters sealed
And sent their sergeants and servants on their way.   2245
Before two weeks had passed
So many men arrived and assembled
That one could have estimated their number at fifty thousand,
Including good sergeants and armed knights.
They let no one go on foot   2250
In order to hurry and save Rome.
I do not know what to say about their travels.
They crossed the Saint Bernard Pass, which was very difficult,
And did not stop until they reached Rome.
But they could not enter the gate   2255
Because the German prevented them from doing so.
King Louis had his tent pitched,
Along with smaller tents and pavilions for his men,
And the kitchens prepared and the cooking fires lit.
Count William led the foragers   2260
Across the land to lay waste
And pillage it.
As a result the army became rich and well provisioned.

56.
Count William led forth the foragers again.
Guy the German rose to his feet   2265
And spoke to a peer of Rome:

"Ha! Noble lord, hold your peace and listen to me.
Arm up to a thousand knights
Before the Franks pitch their tents,
And let them hear your battle cries. 2270
If you need my help, I shall go with you."
And the peer responded, "It will be done."
They quickly prepared themselves:
They put on their hauberks, laced up their helms,
Girded their swords on, and mounted their horses. 2275
They hung their quartered shields around their necks
And took their sharp spears in their hands.
They quickly exited the city by the gate.
A thick fog began to settle in
So that no one could see or ride. 2280
Now the French could not defend themselves
When the Romans descended on their tents.
They took the steeds, killed the squires,
Took the provisions from the kitchen,
And killed the master of provisions. 2285
Louis fled on foot,
Going from one tent to another to hide,
Screaming, "Bertrand, William, where are you?
Sons of barons, help me!
So help me God, I really need it now." 2290
Valiant William led forth the foragers.
His nephew, Count Bertrand, spoke first:
"Uncle William, think about taking action,
For I hear great cries coming from our army.
So help me God, they really need our aid!" 2295
The count answered, "We have to ride
Toward Rome with our strong helms laced up.
If we can surround them and keep them outside the city
Our men will have time to rearm themselves;
We can have great spoils there, 2300
Greater than we have seen since the death of Gaifier."
Bertrand responded, "It will be done."
They began to ride toward Rome
As the thick fog surrounded them.

Now the Romans could not defend themselves 2305
As William began to cry out:
"Monjoie!" he yelled, "strike hard, knights!"
There you would have seen a terrible battle begin,
So many lances broken, so many shields pierced,
So many hauberks torn apart and shattered to pieces; 2310
And the dying tripping and falling upon dead.
Those in William's army put on their hauberks
And encircled the enemy on the front and from behind.
They wanted to leave no one from Rome
Who was not killed and torn to pieces, 2315
Or bound and taken prisoner.
Their lord fled to a hill as fast as possible
And Count William quickly followed him.
He cried out to him, "Come back here, knight,
Or you will soon die like a coward." 2320
He stuck his blade in the side of the duke's hauberk
And he fell forward on his horse's neck.
He drew his sword and was going to cut off his head
When the duke pleaded and begged for mercy:
"Baron, don't kill me if you are William, 2325
But take me alive, I am worth much to you that way!
I shall give you a barrelful of money."
Count William approached him
And the duke gave him his bright, steel blade.
William gave him to Louis as a prisoner, 2330
Then returned to his foragers.
Back in Rome, Guy the German rose to his feet
And said to his men, "Hear me now, be quiet!
My men are dead, killed and torn to pieces.
If I cannot do battle 2335
One on one against a knight,
Then all our efforts are worth nothing."

57.
Guy the German called a messenger,
Had him mount an Arabian steed,
Hung a large marten skin around his neck, 2340

And hastily put a small staff in his hands.
Guy the German gave him the message:
"Go quickly to those silken tents
And tell Louis, the son of Charlemagne,
That he is very wrong to want to destroy my borderlands. 2345
He has no rightful claim to Rome or any of her lands,
And if he wishes to take it by his arrogance,
He will have to fight me,
Or have another knight fight in his place.
And if I am defeated in battle, 2350
He will have Rome and her surrounding lands.
No one will do him harm.
But if I should vanquish him by my sharp sword,
He will not have a penny's worth.
Then he must return to France, to Paris or Chartres, 2355
And leave me Rome, for it is my inheritance."
The messenger responded, "It is right that I do so."
Then he left by the main gate
And rode directly to Louis's camp.
He dismounted near the large silken tent 2360
And entered it,
Where he found Louis, the son of Charlemagne.
He called to him in front of all the barons:
"Just emperor, hear what I have to say!
I do not greet you, for it is not proper that I do so. 2365
Guy the German sends me as his messenger.
Through me, he sends you word—I cannot hide it from you—
That you have no right to Rome or its surrounding lands.
If, in your arrogance, you want to take them,
You will have to fight him 2370
Or have another knight fight in your place.
And if he is defeated in battle,
You will have Rome and her surrounding lands;
No one will do you harm.
But if he should win by his sharp sword, 2375
You will not have a penny's worth;
You must return to Chartres or mighty Paris.
You will leave him Rome, for it is his inheritance."

Hearing this, the king looked down,
And when he lifted his gaze again he spoke to his barons: 2380
"Lord barons, hear what I have to say.
Guy the German makes an outrageous demand of me:
That we have a hand-to-hand combat.
But I am young and of a tender age
And cannot protect my inheritance.   2385
Is there a Frank who will fight in my place?"
When they heard it, they lowered their faces.
Seeing this, the king nearly went mad with anger
And wept softly beneath his marten pelt.
Behold William Fierebrace   2390
Who had led the foragers to that place.
He entered the silken tent completely armed
And beheld the king who was weeping hard;
Seeing this, he nearly went mad with anger.
Then he cried out in front of all the barons: 2395
"Ha! Poor Louis, may God punish you!
Why are you crying? Who has harmed you?"
And Louis did not hesitate to answer:
"By God, lord, I cannot hide it from you:
Guy the German makes an outrageous demand of me.   2400
He wants a hand-to-hand combat with me,
But there is no Frank who will fight in my place,
For I am young and of tender age
And cannot fight as a baron."
—"King," said William, "may God punish you!   2405
For love of you, I have waged twenty-four combats.
Do you think that I shall fail you now in this one?
By God, of course not! I shall fight this battle.
All your Franks are worth nothing."
When he saw the messenger, he spoke harshly to him: 2410

58.
"Friend, fair brother," said noble William,
"Go and tell Guy the German
That a knight who defends his lord
Wishes to do battle—in fact, really desires it!

I shall choose the hostages I want, 2415
And he will take the ones he wants
So that the agreement will be kept for the one who wins."
Paladin Count Bertrand rose to his feet:
"Uncle," he said, "this is not good for us.
All battles and combats have gone to you, 2420
And your valor puts ours to shame.
My lord, I ask for this battle;
With your permission, give it to me."
Count William answered, "You speak foolishly.
When Louis was in despair earlier, 2425
There was no bold or strong person
Who dared offer to fight for him.
Do you think I'm going to back down now?
I shall not for all the gold in the Orient!
Brother messenger, tell Guy the German 2430
That he should arm himself and present himself on the battlefield,
That Count William will meet him there."
The messenger spurred and rode
From there to Rome without wasting any time.
Guy the German came out to meet him: 2435
"Friend, fair brother, what did you learn from the French?"
The messenger answered, "I shall hide nothing:
A knight from the French army
Wants this battle, it's his great desire.
He strongly insists on hostages 2440
And says that you too can take as many as you want.
In this way the winner will be guaranteed the agreement.
I believe his name is William.
Another knight, Bertrand, stood up;
He's William's nephew, I know for sure, 2445
And he really wanted the battle."
—"Friend, fair brother," said brave Guy,
"When I have finished with William on the battlefield,
If his nephew Bertrand wishes,
He will not have far to look for a battle. 2450
Bring me my best armor."
And the messenger replied, "As you wish."

They brought his armor right away.
They helped him put on his Arabian-style hauberk,
Its chain mail as red as a blazing fire,   2455
And laced up his bright green-gold helm
With a carbuncle at the front on the nose guard.
Guy attached his sword on his left side,
Then they brought him his rapid steed.
He hung another sword on the front of the saddle   2460
And mounted his horse
Without using the stirrup or the saddle horn.
He hung his heavy strong shield around his neck,
And in his hands he held a sharp spear
To which his gonfalon was attached by five nails.   2465
He spurred ahead through the gate;
He came riding to Nero's Meadow.
Count William saw him first
And called to Guielin and Bertrand:
"I see my enemy entering the field;   2470
If I wait any longer, he will think I'm a coward.
Bring me my best armor."
And they answered, "As you wish."
They brought it to him right away.
Brave Louis helped with arming him.   2475
He put on his hauberk, laced his bright helm,
And attached Joyous on his left side,
The sword the warrior Charlemagne had given him.
They brought him rapid Alion,
Which he mounted with ease.   2480
He hung around his neck his heavy strong shield
And in his hands he held a sharp spear
To which his gonfalon was attached by five nails.
He spurred ahead through the camp,
Not stopping until he reached the knoll.   2485

59.
Marquis William ascended the knoll;
Guy the German called to him:
"Who are you, don't lie,

You who have a heart so bold
That you would dare come to this field to meet me?"   2490
—"Indeed," said William, "I will tell you right away:
I am William, the son of Count Aymeri
Of Narbonne, the brave and bold one.
I've come to fight you with my sharp steel blade.
Rome belongs rightfully to King Charles of Saint-Denis,   2495
And after him Louis will hold it.
I myself had a battle
At this very place with Corsolt the Arab,
The strongest man who was ever born of woman.
He cut off the nose on my face."   2500
When Guy heard this, he nearly went out of his mind;
He did not want to be there for all the wealth of Paris.
He looked at William and spoke to him:
"Are you that marquis William,
From Narbonne and son of Count Aymeri?   2505
Let's make peace and be good friends,
And you and I shall hold Rome together."
—"Scoundrel!" said William, "God curse you!
I did not come here to talk.
I do not wish to shame my rightful lord;   2510
I would not do it even if I were torn to pieces!"
When Guy heard this, he nearly went out of his mind.
He swore by the blessed apostle:
"I consider myself vile for having made this offer
And now defy you in the name of God of paradise."   2515
And William responded, "And I you!"
They moved away from one another farther than a bow could shoot,
And then they turned and stared at one another.
They held their strong shields in front of their chests
And prepared to strike each other with harsh blows.   2520
They jabbed their steeds with their sharp spurs
And quickly attacked each other with lowered lances.
They exchanged great blows on their rounded shields
Beneath the bosses and smashed and shattered them,
But they could not break through the shiny hauberks.   2525
Not being able to absorb the shock, their lances shattered,

And the pieces went flying high in the air.
Their bodies and chests clashed
As their strong rounded shields came together,
As did their hauberks and prized steeds. 2530
They caused their helms to grind against their faces,
And blood and sweat gushed out.
The two riders and their steeds fell.
While the horses were still on the ground,
The vassals jumped to their feet 2535
With swords drawn and their shields up.
They would soon show that they were not friends!

60.
Count William jumped to his feet
And called on God, the divine avenger:
"Holy Mary, blessed Virgin, help me. 2540
No man has ever unhorsed me."
Guy the German responded haughtily:
"By God, William, that's not worth a penny!
I claim Rome, its walls and its fiefs;
Louis will never inherit them." 2545
—"Foul wretch," said William, "may God destroy you!
By the apostle whom the palmers venerate,
Before nightfall this very day
I believe that I shall rearrange your body
To such an extent that no one would give a cent for you." 2550
He held Joyous with its steel blade
And lunged at Guy ferociously,
Striking him on his green-gold helm
And causing the decorations and gems to fly off.
Were it not for his bright lined hauberk, 2555
Guy would have been useless after the blow.
The blow landed just on his hip
And took off more than a foot of flesh
And exposed the bone above the groin.
"Indeed," said William, "that blow has drawn blood! 2560
Now you know how my steel blade slices."
Guy the German responded haughtily:

"Ha! William, may God destroy you!
Do you think you can scare me with such a small thing?
One is burdened with too much flesh anyway.   2565
But by the cross that palmers venerate,
Before nightfall this very day
I believe I shall avenge my flesh by taking some of yours."
He held his sword with its steel blade
And lunged at William ferociously,   2570
Striking him in the middle of his green-gold helm
And causing the decorations and gems to fly off.
Were it not for his bright lined hauberk,
Count Aymeri would have been without an heir.
But God would not allow or grant it.   2575
Guy did not gain much from this blow,
But instead broke his sword at the handle.
He quickly drew the other one.
Seeing this, William let out a loud laugh
And held Joyous with its rich steel blade   2580
And lunged at Guy ferociously,
Striking him hard on his green-gold helm.
The blow penetrated his shoulder
And sliced all the way down to his foot.
With this blow, he struck him dead.   2585
The Tiber was close by, and he threw his body in it.
The metal he was wearing dragged him to the bottom
So that no one ever retrieved his body.
Seeing this, William began to cry out:
"Monjoie!" he yelled, "so help me, St. Denis!   2590
King Louis is avenged of this one."
He mounted his horse, Alion,
And took Clinevent, which he did not wish to leave behind.
He wasted no time in returning to the tents.
Count Bertrand, his nephew, came out to meet him,   2595
Along with Louis, full of joy and happiness.
Gautier and Guielin wept profusely,
For they had never known such fear under heaven
Except for the day William had fought against Corsolt:
"Uncle William, are you safe and sound?"   2600

—"Yes," he said, "thank God in heaven!
Fair nephew Bertrand, I shall not hide it from you,
I give you now this rapid steed
Because you requested the battle yesterday."
Bertrand responded, "Many thanks!"   2605
There was only fear among the people in Rome.
They said one to another, "We're doomed.
Our lord is dead and massacred,
And we must now humbly submit.
Let us go quickly and beg for mercy!"   2610
They said one to another, "This is what we must do."
With large precious gold crosses,
With phylacteries, incense, and psalters,
They carried out the relics from the church.
They opened the gates right away   2615
And welcomed their rightful lord.

61.
William, the noble knight, entered Rome.
He took his lord right away
And had him sit on the throne;
He crowned him in the name of the French barons.   2620
There they all swore to him an oath,
Both those who were faithful   2621a
And those who were not loyal,
As you will hear before the setting of the sun.

62.
Brave William entered Rome
And crowned his lord, Louis.   2625
He assured him of all the empire.
Then he made preparations to leave.
William and his men rode and traveled so hard together
That they arrived in the kingdom of France.
The king went to the city of Paris;   2630
Count William went to Montreuil by the Sea.
Now William thought he would be able to rest,
Hunting in the woods and fishing in the rivers.

But this was not to last long,
Because the French began to revolt   2635
And act like fools and fight with one another;
They burned the towns and destroyed the land
And did not want to protect Louis.
A messenger went to tell William;
Hearing this, William nearly lost his mind.   2640
He called to Bertrand, "Lord nephew, listen to me.
For the love of God, what advice do you offer me?
The king, my lord, is completely disinherited."
Bertrand responded, "Just let him be.
Let's abandon France and leave it to the devil,   2645
Along with this king who is such a fool.
Soon he will not have even a foot of his inheritance."
William responded, "Abandon that idea!
I wish to spend my youth in his service."
He called up all his men and his friends;   2650
They rode and traveled so hard
That they arrived in the city of Paris;
There William found King Louis.
From that day forward there was constant war.
When short-nosed William saw   2655
That Louis could not remain in this land
Because he had too many mortal enemies here,
He took the child that he had to protect
And brought him to the city of Laon.
He made those in the city watch after Louis   2660
While he burned and pillaged the surrounding lands.
Thus he cut through the main lines of defense
And pierced through and toppled the high walls.
In a year, he had pressed them so much
That he made fifteen counts come to court   2665
And do fealty for their lands
Before King Louis, who was to reign over France.
And he gave Louis his sister in marriage.
Louis was surrounded now with many barons,
But when he became powerful, he was not grateful to William.   2670

2

The Convoy to Nîmes

1.

Listen, my lords: may glorious God,
The king of majesty, increase your virtue!
Would it please you to hear a good song
About the best man who ever believed in God?
It is about William, the short-nosed marquis,   5
How he captured Nîmes with filled carts,
Then conquered the stronghold of Orange,
And had Guibourc baptized and christened
After he captured her from the pagan King Tibaut.
Then he took her as his wife and spouse,   10
And killed Corsolt in the fields outside Rome.
He greatly exalted holy Christendom.
He accomplished so much on earth that he is crowned in heaven.[1]
It was in May, in the early summer:
The woods were coming into leaf, the meadows turning green,   15
The birds were singing beautifully and sweetly.
Count William was returning from the hunt
In a forest where he had been for a long while.
He had caught two plump stags

---

1   Lines 6–13 provide a summary of *The Convoy to Nîmes*, *The Conquest of Orange*, and *The Coronation of Louis*. Though mentioned last here, the events of *The Coronation of Louis* come first in William's fictional biography.

And had them packed up and loaded onto three Spanish mules.   20
The valiant man had four arrows at his side;
From the hunt he had brought back his bow of laburnum wood.
He was accompanied by forty young men,
Sons of counts and landed princes;
They were newly dubbed knights.   25
They had hawks for hunting,
And brought packs of hounds with them.
They entered Paris by the Petit Pont.
Count William was very noble and valiant:
He had his venison brought to his lodgings.   30
On the way he met Bertrand
And asked him, "Lord nephew, where are you coming from?"
Bertrand replied, "You will hear the truth:
From the palace, where I stayed a long while;
I heard and listened to a great deal of talk.   35
Our emperor has provided his barons with fiefs:
To one he gave land, to another a castle, to another a stronghold,
To another a town, as he saw fit.
You and I, uncle, are forgotten.
It doesn't matter to me, for I am a young man,   40
But it does matter to you, my lord, who are so valiant
And have suffered and taken such pains,
Staying awake by night and fasting by day."
When William heard this, he burst out laughing.
"Nephew," said the count, "let it be.   45
Go quickly to your lodgings
And get yourself handsomely equipped,
And I shall go talk to Louis."
Bertrand said, "Lord, just as you command."
He returned quickly to his lodgings.   50
Count William was very noble and valiant;
He did not stop until he reached the palace.
He dismounted under the thick branches of the olive tree,
Then climbed the marble staircase.
He stomped so vigorously on the floor   55
That he split open the tops of his leather boots.
Every baron there was terrified.

The king saw him and rose to meet him;
Then he said to him, "William, now sit down."
—"I will not, lord," said valiant William,   60
"But I would like to have a word with you."
Louis said, "As you wish.
I believe you will be well heard."
—"Louis, my brother," said valiant William,
"I have not served you by giving you massages at night,   65
Or by disinheriting widows and children;
Rather, I have served you bravely with my weapons
And fought many fierce battles,
Where I have killed many a noble young man,
Thus causing sin to enter me.   70
Whoever they were, God created them.
May God preserve their souls and grant me pardon!"
—"Lord William," said valiant Louis,
"If you please, be patient for a while.
Winter will pass, summer will return;   75
One of these days, one of your peers will die.
I shall give you all of his land
And his wife, if you wish to take her."
Hearing this, William nearly went out of his mind.
"God!" said the count, "who suffered on the cross,   80
What a long wait for a poor young man
Who has nothing for himself and nothing to give others!
I need to feed my horse,
But have no idea how I shall manage.
God! What a deep valley he must descend,   85
And what a steep hill he must climb,
The man who awaits the death of another to enrich himself!"

2.
"God!" said William, "what a long wait
For a young man my age,
Who has nothing to give and nothing for his own use.   90
I must find food for my horse,
But I have no idea where to find the oats.
Are you surprised, king, that I complain?"

3.

"Louis, my lord," said proud William,
"Had I not feared that my peers would call me a traitor,   95
I would have left you a full year ago,
When I received the letter from Spoleto
Sent by the mighty King Gaifier,
Saying that he would give me a quarter of his land,
Or even half, along with his daughter.   100
Then I could have made war on the king of France."
Hearing this, the king thought he would lose his mind.
He said some words that were better left unsaid.
Thus the conflict began to escalate,
And the hostility between them intensified.   105

4.

"Lord William," said King Louis,
"There is no man in this entire country,
Not Gaifier, not the king of Spoleto, nor any other,
Who, if he dared hold even one of my men,
Would not be killed or captured,   110
Or driven out of his land into exile."
—"God!" said the count, "how poorly I am treated here,
Entirely dependent on you for my sustenance.
If I continue to serve you, I should be ashamed!"

5.

"My noble companions," said valiant William,   115
"Go quickly back to our lodgings,
Equip yourselves handsomely,
And load up the packhorses.
I am so angry I must leave the court.
Since we have remained with the king purely for sustenance,   120
He can say he has worked miracles!"
And they responded, "Just as you command."
William climbed up onto a hearth;
He leaned on the bow of laburnum wood
That he had brought back from the hunt   125
With such force that it shattered down the middle,

With pieces flying all the way up to the beams
And then falling right beneath the king's nose.
He began to accuse Louis of a great outrage,
For he had served him well: 130
"Am I now to be reproached for my extensive service,
The great combats and fierce battles?
Louis, my lord," said valiant William,[2]
"Do you not remember the great battle
That I waged for you in the fields outside Rome?   135
There I fought the emir Corsolt,
The strongest man to be found in Christendom
Or in Saracen lands.
With his naked sword he dealt me such a blow
On my helmet adorned with jewels set in gold,   140
That he knocked the crystal to the ground.
He sliced off the nosepiece
And brought down his sword right through my nostrils;
I had to retrieve the tip of my nose with my own two hands;
When it was mended there was a large bump—   145
A curse on the doctor who tended to it!—
This is why they call me 'short-nosed William.'
I am deeply ashamed of it when I am in the company of my peers,
And before the king, in the assembly of lords.
Cursed be anyone who received arms from the king: a spear,   150
A lance, a shield, a shod palfrey,
Or a steel sword with its pommel!"

6.
"King Louis," said wise William,
"Rightful emperor, you are the son of Charlemagne,
The best king ever to bear arms,   155
The proudest and the most just.
King, now remember the fierce battle
I waged for you at the Pierrelate ford:
I captured Dagobert, who has since remained with you.
See him there with his fine marten furs;   160

---

2   Lines 134–251 summarize key episodes from *The Coronation of Louis*.

If he denies it, he should bear the blame.
After that battle, I waged another for you:
When Charlemagne wanted to make you king,
And the crown was firmly in place on the altar,
You remained for a long time in your seat: 165
The French could see that you were of little worth:
They wanted to make you a cleric, an abbot, or a priest,
Or they would have made you a canon somewhere.
When, in the church of St. Mary Magdalene,
I saw that, because of his powerful lineage, Hernaut   170
Wanted to take the crown for himself,
I was not pleased one bit;
I dealt him such a great blow
That I knocked him to the ground, on the marble floor.
For this I incurred the hatred of his powerful family.   175
I came forward through the entire court,
So that all could see,
Including the pope and all the patriarchs.
I took the crown; you left with it on your head.
Of this service you clearly have no memory,   180
Since you distributed your lands without thinking of me."

7.
"Louis, my lord," said brave William,
"Do you not remember the arrogant scoundrel
Who came to defy you right here in your own court?
'You have no right to France,' he said in front of everyone. 185
In your empire you didn't have a single baron,
Rightful emperor, who would speak up for you at all.
Mindful of my legitimate lord,
I came forward and did something reckless:
I tied him to a stake like a traitor.   190
The time would come when I'd pay for it:
As I was returning from Mont-Saint-Michel,
I met old, red-headed Richard,
The father of that arrogant Norman.
He had twenty men, and I had but two.   195
I drew my sword bravely;

With my naked sword I killed seven of their men,
And before their eyes I brought down their lord.
I delivered him to you at your court in Paris;
He later died in your great tower.   200
Of this service you clearly remember little,
Since you granted fiefs without thinking of me.
King, remember Guy the German:
While you were traveling to the church of St. Peter,
He challenged your right to the French, the Burgundians,   205
The crown, and the city of Laon.
I fought with him in the presence of many barons;
Right through his body I ran my lance with the gonfalon,
And I threw him in the Tiber, where he was eaten by fish.
I would have thought myself a fool for doing this,   210
Had it not been for my host Guion,
Who put me out to sea in a large ship.
King, remember Oton's great army?
With you were Frenchmen, Burgundians,
Lotharingians, Flemish, and Frisians.   215
You made your way across the Saint Bernard Pass and Montbardon
All the way to Rome, to the place known as Nero's Meadow.
I myself put up your tent
And then served you sumptuous venison."

8.
"When you had finished eating,   220
I approached you to take my leave.
Gladly and willingly you gave me permission,
Thinking I was going to bed
In my tent, to comfort my weary body.
Instead I assembled two thousand mounted knights   225
And came to keep watch behind your tent
In a wood of pine and laurel trees:
There, I had the barons hide and wait.
You didn't deign to watch for the Romans;
Over fifteen thousand of them had mounted their horses.   230
They came to your tent to hurl spears,
To rip the cords and overturn your tents,

To pull up your tablecloths and scatter your food.
I saw them capture your seneschal and your gatekeeper;
You were fleeing on foot from one tent to another   235
Through the crush of the fight like a pitiful dog,
Crying at the top of your voice:
'Bertrand! William! Come help me!'
Then, noble king, I truly pitied you.
There I fought with seven thousand mighty warriors,   240
And I conquered for you
Over three hundred knights with their swift steeds.
I saw their lord hiding behind a marble column;
I recognized him instantly by his fine ridged helmet
With its carbuncle gleaming on the nosepiece.   245
I dealt him such a blow with my sharp spear
That I knocked him onto his horse's neck.
He begged for mercy, which stirred my pity:
'Baron, if you truly are William, don't kill me!'
I brought him to you without delay.   250
Because of this, you still rule in Rome.
Now you are powerful and I am little esteemed.
For as long as I have served you, I have protected you,
Without gaining a penny for myself.
And so no one at court considers me a knight."   255

9.
"Louis, my lord," continued William,
"I have served you so long that my hair has turned white,
Without gaining a whit for myself
Nor wearing finer attire at court.
I don't even have a house of my own.   260
Louis, my lord, have you lost your senses?
People used to say that I was in your closest circle.
I used to ride fine horses with flowing manes;
I served you in fields and marshes.
No one was ever better off.   265
I never even had a nick in my shield
Unless it was caused by an enemy lance!
I killed more than twenty thousand faithless Turks;

But, by the one who dwells in heaven on high,
I shall turn against my lord. 270
You can remove me from that circle of friends!"

10.
"God," said William, "born of the holy Virgin,
Why did I kill so many fair young men
And why did I sadden so many mothers,
Committing sins that still remain on my soul? 275
I have served this wretched king of France for so long,
Without gaining anything worth the blade of a lance."

11.
"Lord William," said valiant Louis,
"By the apostle they pray to in Nero's Meadow,
There are still sixty of your peers 280
To whom I have promised and given nothing."
William replied, "Noble king, that is a lie.
I have no peers in Christendom,
Except you, who wear the crown;
I do not mean to place myself above you. 285
Now take those men you just mentioned
And lead them one by one into this meadow,
On their horses, well equipped and prepared;
If I don't kill all those men and more,
Let me never take any part of your inheritance. 290
I include you in their number as well, if you'd like."
Hearing this, the king bowed toward William.
When he straightened up, he said to him:

12.
"Lord William," said noble Louis,
"Now I see clearly that you are very angry." 295
—"Truly I am," said William, "as were my kinsmen.
So it goes when a man serves a bad lord:
The more he does, the less he gains.
Everything just keeps getting worse for him."

13.
"Lord William," said brave Louis,   300
"Now I see clearly that you are quite angry."
—"Truly I am," said William, "as were my ancestors.
So it goes when a man serves a bad lord;
The more he lifts him up, the less he gains himself."
—"Lord William," Louis replied,   305
"You have protected and served me faithfully,
More than any man in my court.
Come forward, I shall give you a fine gift:
Take the land belonging to the brave Count Foucon;
You will have three thousand men to serve you."   310
—"I will not, my lord," William replied.
"The noble count has two sons
Who are perfectly capable of maintaining that fief.
Give me another; I have no use for this one."

14.
"Lord William," said King Louis,   315
"Since you do not wish to accept this land
And do not want to take it from the count's children,
Take Auberi the Burgundian's land
And his stepmother Hermensant of Tori,
The best woman who ever drank wine;   320
You will have three thousand armed knights to serve you."
—"I will not, lord," replied William.
"The noble count has a son;
His name is Robert, but he is still quite small.
He still doesn't know how to dress himself or put on his shoes.   325
If, God willing, he grows up strong and robust,
He will be perfectly capable of maintaining the fief."

15.
"Lord William," said brave Louis,
"Since you do not want to disinherit that child,
Take the marquis Berengier's land.   330
The count is dead; take his wife as well.
You will have two thousand knights to serve you

With their shining armor and rapid horses.
They will not cost you a penny."
Hearing this, William thought he would lose his mind.   335
In a clear voice, he began to shout:
"Listen to me, noble knights!
Hear how Louis, my rightful lord,
Compensates those who serve him willingly.
Now let me tell you about the marquis Berengier: 340
He was born in the Val de Riviers;
He killed a count and was unable to pay the fine.[3]
He fled to the royal palace in Laon,
And there he fell at the emperor's feet.
The emperor received him willingly,   345
Gave him land and a courtly wife.
He served the emperor unfailingly for a long time.
Then it came about that the emperor waged war
On the Saracens, the Turks, and the Slavs.
The battle was terrible and fierce;   350
The king was thrown from his horse.
He would never have been able to mount again
If the marquis Berengier had not appeared.
Berengier saw his lord struggling in the fray;
He galloped there at full speed,   355
Wielding his sword of burnished steel.
There he slaughtered all around him like a boar among dogs,
Then dismounted from his rapid steed
To assist and rescue his lord.
The king mounted his horse with Berengier holding the stirrup,   360
And then fled like a cowardly cur.
The marquis Berengier remained on the battlefield;
There we saw him killed and cut to pieces,
And we could neither help nor assist him.
He left a noble heir   365
Called young Berengier.

---

3   The Salic law of the Franks allowed for compensation or blood money (*Wergeld*) to be paid to the surviving family.

Anyone who wants to harm this child is completely crazy,
And a faithless traitor, so help me God.
The emperor wishes to give me his fief:
I will have none of it, and I want all of you to hear me!   370
And there is one thing I want you to know:
By the apostle they seek in Rome,
Anyone in all of France, no matter how bold,
Who takes young Berengier's land,
Will at once have his head severed by my sword!"   375
—"Many thanks, my lord!" said the knights
Who served the young Berengier.
There were a hundred of them bowing to William
And clinging to his legs and feet.
"Lord William," said Louis, "listen: 380
Since this domain does not suit you,
So help me God, I shall now give you a fief
That will elevate your position, if you are reasonable.
I shall give you a quarter of France:
A quarter of the abbeys and a quarter of the markets,   385
A quarter of the cities and a quarter of the archbishoprics,
A quarter of the men-at-arms and a quarter of the knights,
A quarter of the vavasors and a quarter of the footmen,
A quarter of the maidens and a quarter of the women,
And a quarter of the priests and a quarter of the churches;   390
From my stables I give you a quarter of the horses;
From my treasury I give you a quarter of the money;
I willingly grant you a quarter
Of the whole empire that I govern.
Accept this, noble knight."   395
—"I will not, lord," replied William.
"Not for all the gold beneath the heavens,
For then these valiant knights would say:
'Behold William, the proud-faced marquis,
See how he deceived his rightful lord!   400
The king gave him half of his kingdom,
And William paid not a penny for it.
He has truly slashed his lord's revenue.'"

16.

"Lord William," said valiant Louis,
"By the apostle they seek in Nero's Meadow,   405
Since you do not wish to accept this fief,
I don't know what on earth I can give you,
And I cannot think of another domain to offer."
—"King," said William, "let it be, then.
For the moment, I do not wish to speak of this any further.   410
When it pleases you, you will give me many
Castles and provinces, fortresses and strongholds."
Having said this, the count turned away.
He strode down the steps angrily.
On his way he met Bertrand,   415
Who asked him, "Lord, my uncle, where are you coming from?"
And William said, "You will hear the truth:
From the palace, where I stayed a long while.
I argued and quarreled with Louis:
I have served him faithfully, but he has given me nothing."   420
And Bertrand said, "By God's curse!
You should not provoke your rightful lord,
But rather serve and honor him,
Protect and defend him against all who would harm him!"
—"Enough!" replied William, "He has led me along   425
So that I have spent my whole life serving him,
Without gaining so much as a peeled egg."

17.

And William said, "Lord Bertrand, fair nephew,
I have spent all my time serving the king,
Using my strength to elevate and exalt him.   430
Now he has granted me a quarter of France
As if it were a reproach.
In exchange for my service he wants to pay me;
But, by the apostle they seek in Rome,
I intend to knock the crown off his head: 435
I put it there, and I want to remove it."
Bertrand said, "Lord, you are not speaking as a valiant knight.
You should not threaten your rightful lord,

But rather elevate and exalt him,
Help and assist him against all who would harm him." 440
And the count replied, "You are right, fair nephew;
One should always value loyalty.
Thus commands God, who judges all things."

18.
"Uncle William," said wise Bertrand,
"Let us go speak to Louis, 445
You and I, in that vast palace,
To request a gift I have thought about carefully."
—"What would that be?" asked valiant William.
And Bertrand replied, "You will hear the truth:
Ask him for the kingdom of Spain, 450
Tortolouse and Portpaillart by the Sea,
And also Nîmes, that fine city,
And then Orange, so worthy of praise.
If he grants you all this, no need to thank him,
For he never bore a shield in those places 455
Or enlisted knights there in his service.
He can easily give you this territory
Without doing any harm to his kingdom."
Hearing this, William burst out laughing.
"Nephew," said William, "you were born under a lucky star, 460
For I too had the same thought,
But I wanted to speak with you about it first."
They took each other by the hand and went up to the palace,
Not stopping until they reached the great hall.
Seeing them, the king rose to meet them, 465
And then said, "William, please be seated."
—"I will not, lord," said the well-born count.
"But I would like to speak with you briefly
To request a gift I have thought about carefully."
And the king said, "Blessed be God! 470
If you want a castle, fortified city,
Tower, town, or stronghold,
I shall willingly grant it to you.
If you want to take half my kingdom,

I willingly bestow it upon you, lord,   475
For I have always found you to be most faithful,
And it is because of you that I am proclaimed king of France."
Hearing this, William burst out laughing.
He stood before the king and spoke to him thus:
"I will never seek such a gift.   480
Rather, I am asking you for the kingdom of Spain,
And Tortolouse and Portpaillart by the Sea;
I am also asking you for the city of Nîmes,
And then Orange, so worthy of praise.
If you grant me all this, no need for me to thank you,   485
For you never bore a shield in these places
Or provided sustenance to knights there;
This will in no way diminish your patrimony."
Hearing this, the king burst out laughing.

19.
"Louis, my lord," said strong William,   490
"In God's name, give me all the passes into Spain;
The land will be mine, and the treasure yours;
A thousand knights will accompany you on campaign."

20.
"Give me, lord, the great city of Vaseüre,
And also Nîmes and its stronghold.   495
I shall drive out the evil pagan Otrant,
Who has slain so many Franks needlessly
And forced them to flee many lands.
If God helps me, and if it pleases him,
I shall ask you, lord, for no other land."   500

21.
"Give me, my lord, Valsore and Valsure,
Give me Nîmes with its great pointed towers,
And then Orange, that mighty city,
And the Nîmes countryside with all its pastures,
Where the Rhône flows through the ravines."   505

Louis said, "Lord God, help me!
Can one man alone hold such a fief?"
And William replied, "I have no desire to stay here.
I shall ride at night, by moonlight,
Clothed in my felt-lined hauberk,   510
And I shall cast out the foul race of Saracens."

22.
"Lord William," said the king, "listen:
By the apostle they seek in Nero's Meadow,
The land is not mine; I cannot give it to you.
It is held by Saracens and infidels: 515
Clareau of Orange and his brother Aceré,
And Goliath and King Desramé,
And Arrogant and Morant and Barré,
And Quinzepaumes and his brother Gondrez,
Otrant of Nîmes and King Murgalé.[4]   520
King Tibaut is to be crowned there.
He married Orable, the emir's sister.
She is the fairest woman to be found
In any pagan or Christian land.
This is why I fear that if you go up against them,   525
You will not be able to liberate this land.
Please remain here instead.
Let us divide our cities evenly:
You will have Chartres, and leave me Orléans
And the crown, for I desire nothing more."   530
—"I will not, lord," said valiant William,
"For then the noble barons would say:
'Behold William, the short-nosed marquis,
See how he has overshadowed his rightful lord:
The king gave him half his kingdom,   535
And William pays not a penny in return.
He has truly diminished his lord's revenue.'"

---

4   The names given to Saracen adversaries often sound exotic to the French ear, or may connote
evil or monstrosity.

23.

"Lord William," said the king, "noble warrior,
What do you care about unjust reproaches?
I do not want you to abandon me here in this land.   540
You will have Chartres, and leave me Orléans
And the crown, for I ask nothing more of you."
—"I will not, lord," replied William;
"Not for all the gold beneath the heavens.
I do not wish to diminish your realm,   545
But rather increase it by the blade of my sword;
You are my lord, and I do not wish to harm you.
Do you not know why I wish to leave you?   547a
It was at Michaelmas;
I went to Saint-Gilles, and came back by way of Montpellier.
A courtly knight gave me lodging;   550
He gave me plenty to eat and drink,
And he provided hay and oats for my swift charger.
When we had eaten,
The noble knight went to amuse himself in the meadow
With his entourage.   555
I was about to go on my way   555a
When his wife seized my horse by the reins.
I dismounted, and she held my stirrup.
Then she led me down into a cellar,
And from the cellar to an upper room.
Before I realized it, she had fallen at my feet.   560
I thought, my lord, that she sought my affection
Or other things that women seek from men.
If I had known, I would not have gone near her
For a thousand pounds.
I asked her: 'My lady, my good woman, what do you want?'   565
—'Have mercy, William, noble knight!' she said,
'I beg you to take pity on this land,
For the love of God who was hung on the cross!'
She made me put my head out the window;
I saw the land full of pagan devils   570
Burning cities and violating churches,
Destroying chapels and overturning bell towers,

Twisting the breasts of courtly women.
My heart was filled with great pity;
I wept tenderly, the tears streaming from my eyes.   575
Then and there, I pledged to glorious God in heaven,
And to St. Giles, to whom I had just prayed,
That I would help the people of this land
With as many troops as I could command."

24.

"Lord William," said noble Louis,   580
"Since you have no interest in the land I have offered,
God help me, I am distressed and sorrowful.
Noble knight, come forward;
I shall agree to everything you have asked.
With this glove, take Spain as your fief;[5]   585
I give it to you under one condition:
If it causes you pain or anguish,
I will not protect you here or elsewhere."
And William replied, "And I ask for nothing more
Than your help once in seven years."   590
Louis said, "I grant this willingly.
Truly, I shall do as you wish."
—"Many thanks, my lord," said the count, "now let's see."
Count William looked around him.
He saw Guielin and Bertrand standing there;   595
They were his nephews, sons of Bernard of Brabant.
He called to them loudly, for all to hear:
"Come forward, Guielin and Bertrand!
You are my friends and my close relatives;
Present yourselves before the king;   600
For this fief that I hereby request,
Receive the glove along with me.
We shall share both the benefits and the hardships."
Hearing this, Guielin smiled deceitfully,
And said softly so that none could hear: 605
"I shall make my uncle very unhappy."

---

5   The glove was a symbol of investiture, and often accompanied the granting of a fief.

—"You will not, sir," said Count Bertrand,
"For valiant William is quite fierce."
—"What do I care?" said noble Guielin,
"I am very young, only twenty years old;   610
I cannot yet suffer pain and hardship."
Hearing this, his father, Bernard of Brabant,
Nearly lost his mind.
He lifted his hand and struck him hard.
"There! Foolish fiend, now you have made me angry!   615
Present yourself at once before the king.
By the apostle the penitents seek,
If you do not receive the glove with William,
This sword will deal you such a nasty blow
That from this day forward no doctor   620
Will be able to heal you for the rest of your life.
Go in search of a fief, since you have none,
Just as I did in my youth.
For, by the apostle the penitents seek,
You shall never have the smallest parcel of my domain.   625
I shall bestow it upon anyone I please."
Guielin and Bertrand came forward
And climbed onto a table.
With clear, loud voices they shouted,
"Lord Bernard of Brabant has beaten us!   630
But by the apostle the penitents seek,
The Saracens and Persians will pay for this dearly.
They will realize that they are in for a very bad year;
They will die by the hundreds and thousands!"

25.
William climbed onto a table.   635
With his loud, clear voice he began to shout:
"Hear me, barons of France!
God help me, I can boast of this:
I have more land than thirty of my peers,
Though I have not yet liberated any portion of it.   640
I say this to the poor young men
With crippled old horses and tattered clothing,

Who have served without gaining a thing:
If they wish to prove themselves in battle with me,
I shall give them money and estates,   645
Castles and borderlands, fortresses and strongholds,
If they help me conquer this land
And exalt and elevate Christianity.
I want to say this to the poor young men,
And to the squires in tattered clothing: 650
If they come with me to conquer Spain,
And help me liberate that country
And exalt and elevate Christianity,
I shall give them plenty of money and gleaming silver,
Castles and borderlands, fortresses and strongholds,   655
And Spanish horses, and they will be dubbed knights."

26.

Hearing this, the young men were joyful and glad;
With loud voices, they began to call out:
"Lord William, for God's sake, do not delay!
Those without horses will follow you on foot."   660
You should have seen those poor squires,
And the poor knights along with them!
They went up to William, the proud-faced marquis.
In a short time there were thirty thousand of them,
Equipped with arms according to their means;   665
All of them vowed and swore
That they would not fail him, even if they were torn limb from limb.
Seeing this, the count was joyful and glad;
He thanked them in the name of glorious God.
Count William was most deserving of praise.   670
He went to Louis to take his leave,
Which the king granted willingly and gladly:
"Go, fair lord, in the name of glorious God in heaven!
May glorious Jesus grant you a successful journey
And a safe and sound return!"   675
William set off, the proud-faced marquis,
Accompanied by many noble knights.
In the middle of the great hall old Aymon suddenly appeared—

May glorious God in heaven destroy him!—
Seeing the king, he addressed him at once: 680
"Righteous emperor, how you have been tricked!"
—"In what way, fair lord?" asked Louis.
—"My lord," he said, "I shall explain it to you:
William the warrior is leaving your court,
Accompanied by many noble knights.   685
He has so deprived you of France's finest men
That if war breaks out, you will not be able to defend yourself.
And I firmly believe that he will return on foot;[6]
All the others will be reduced to begging."
—"You speak dishonorably," replied Louis.   690
"William the warrior is a very worthy man.
In no land is there a better knight to be found.
He has served me well by the blade of his sword;
May glorious Jesus grant him a safe return
And allow him to liberate all of Spain!"   695
A noble knight was there,
Called Gautier the Toulousain.
When he heard William being insulted,
He was most distressed and nearly burst with anger.
He came quickly down the stairs of the great hall,   700
Went up to William and grabbed his stirrups,
As well as the reins of his rapid steed.
"My lord," he said, "you are an excellent knight,
But in the palace you are not worth a penny!"
—"Who says so?" asked proud William.   705
—"My lord," he said, "I must not conceal this from you:
By the faith I owe you, it is old Aymon.
He is trying to discredit you in the eyes of the king."
And William said, "He will pay dearly for it.
If God grants me a safe return,   710
I will have him torn limb from limb,
Or hanged on the gallows or drowned!"
And Gautier replied, "I don't care about threats;

---

6   Aymon is most likely predicting that William will lose his horse in battle and be obliged to
return on foot.

Men who threaten are worthless!
Instead, I would ask you to do this: 715
Give him the reward corresponding to his service.
Begin your war here;
Aymon is the first to contest your expedition."
And William said, "What you say is true, by my head!"
The valiant knight dismounted, and Gautier held his stirrup;   720
Hand in hand, they climbed the staircase.
Seeing this, the king rose to meet them.
Wrapping both arms around William's neck,
He kissed him three times with great affection.
He spoke to him most amicably: 725
"Lord William, is there anything you desire
That I can procure for you with gold or silver?
If so, you shall have it, without difficulty."
— "Many thanks, my lord," replied William.
"I have all that I need.   730
But I would like to ask you for one thing:
Never take a scoundrel as your counsellor."
Then Lord William looked behind him;
In the middle of the great hall he spied old Aymon.
Seeing him, he began to insult him: 735
"Ah! wretched scoundrel, may God destroy you!
Why do you strive to condemn a noble man
When I never in my life harmed you in any way?
Yet you take pains to slander me?
By St. Denis, to whom we pray,   740
Before you leave, I plan to make you pay dearly!"
He came forward, and when he had rolled up his sleeves,
He grabbed Aymon by the hair with his left hand
And, raising his right hand, struck him in the neck,
Breaking his nape in two;   745
He knocked him dead right at his feet.
Count William grabbed him by the head,
And Gautier the Toulousain by his legs,
Together they flung him out the window into the orchard
On top of an apple tree, breaking him in two.   750
"Away with you!" they cried. "Wretched scoundrel;

You will never again make a penny from your lies!"
—"Louis, my lord," said proud William,
"Never believe scoundrels or slanderers,
For your father never held them in any esteem.   755
I shall go off to campaign in Spain;
The land will be yours, my lord, if I conquer it."
—"Go, fair lord, in the name of God in heaven.
May glorious Jesus grant you a successful journey,
And may I see you again, safe and sound and whole!"   760
William set off, the proud-faced marquis,
In the company of many princes,
And Guielin and Bertrand, his nephews.
They brought along three hundred packhorses.
I can tell you what the first one carried: 765
Golden chalices and missals and psalters,
Silken copes and crosses and censers;
When they arrive in the devastated realm,
They will all first serve the Lord.

27.
I can tell you what the second one carried: 770
Vessels of pure gold, missals, and breviaries,
And crucifixes and precious altar cloths;
When they come into the savage realm,
They will be able to serve Jesus, the heavenly One.

28.
I can tell you what the third one carried: 775
Pots and pans, cauldrons and trivets,
And sharp hooks, tongs, and andirons;
Thus when they come to the devastated realm,
They will be able to prepare food,
Serving first William the warrior,   780
And then all of his knights.

29.
William left with his brave company of knights,
And commended to God France, Aix-la-Chapelle,

Paris, Chartres, and all other lands.
They passed by Burgundy, Berry, and Auvergne   785
And arrived one night at the ford before the passes,
Where they pitched their tents and made their camp.

30.
The cooks started fires in the hearths
And began to prepare the meal.
Count William was in his tent;   790
He began to sigh deeply
And to reflect in his innermost being.
Bertrand noticed and began to observe him.
"Dear uncle," he said, "why are you lamenting?
Are you a woman crying about being a widow?"   795
—"Absolutely not, nephew, I am thinking about something else,
About what these valiant knights will say:
'Look at William, the proud-faced marquis,
How he has treated his rightful lord
Who wanted to give him half his kingdom,   800
Yet the foolish count didn't even appreciate it,
But took Spain instead where he had no legitimate claim.'
I shall never again see four people getting together
Without thinking they are talking about me."
—"Uncle William, let this be.   805
Don't be upset about this,
Our future is in God's hands.
Call for water and let's sit down to eat."
—"I shall do so, nephew," said the count.
They signaled the servers to pour the water   810
And sat down together to eat.
There was much meat: wild boar,
Cranes, wild geese, and peacock seasoned with pepper.
And after they had feasted lavishly,
The squires cleared the tables.   815
The knights returned to their lodgings
Until the next day at dawn
When they mounted their warhorses.
They approached the marquis William and asked,

"My lord, what do you think?   820
Tell us which way you want to go."
—"Noble knights, you worry too much.
We just left a short while ago;
We will go straight to Brioude where the saint is honored,
Then to Our Lady of Le Puy,   825
Where we will make an offering
And pray for Christendom."
And they responded, "Just as you wish."
Then they rode out in ordered groups
And crossed the hills and mountains.   830

31.
According to the directions that William gave them,
They crossed Berry and Auvergne;
They passed by Clermont and Montferrand on the right;
They steered clear of the city and its dwellings
Because they did not want to disturb the inhabitants.   835

32.
They slept that night and departed in the morning.
They gathered up the tents, folded the pavilions,
And put their camping gear on the packhorses.
They rode off through the forests and woods,
Passing by Regordane   840
And not stopping until Le Puy.

33.
Count William went to pray in the church
And left three silver marks on the altar,
And four silk cloths and three rugs embroidered with circles.
The princes left very valuable offerings.   845
Never before was there such an offering, nor ever will there be again.
When short-nosed William left the church,
He saw his men and began to speak to them:
"Barons," he said, "listen to me.
This is the border region of the criminal race.   850
From here onward, wherever you go,

Everyone you meet
Will be either a Saracen or a Slav.
Take up arms and mount your horses.
May we plunder, oh noble and renowned knights!   855
If God grants you something, take it.
May the entire country be yours."
And the knights answered, "Just as you wish."
They put on their hauberks, laced up their jeweled helmets,
And belted on their swords with their gold inlaid pommels.   860
They mounted the saddles of their fierce warhorses.
Their mighty bossed shields hung at their sides,
And they carried in their hands their black-enameled spears.
They left the city in ordered formation,
Had the banner carried before them,   865
And headed straight for Nîmes.
What a wonder to see so many sparkling helmets!
The vanguard was led by the renowned Bertrand,
Gautier of Termes, Gilemer the Scot,
And Guielin, the brave and wise.   870
Valiant William led the rear guard,
Made up of ten thousand well-armed Frenchmen,
Ready for battle.
They had not gone more than four leagues
When they encountered in the middle of their route a peasant   875
Coming from Saint-Gilles, where he had stayed;
He had with him four oxen he had bought,
As well as his three children.
The peasant wisely recognized
That salt was expensive in the region where he was born,   880
So he had a barrel on his wagon
That he had filled to the brim with it.
His three children
Were playing and laughing with big pieces of bread in their hands.
They were playing marbles on top of the salt.   885
The French laughed. What else could they do?
Count Bertrand addressed him:
"Tell us, peasant, in the name of your faith, where were you born?"
And the peasant answered, "I shall tell you the truth,

In the name of Mohammed, in Laval-sur-Cler.   890
I am coming from Saint-Gilles, where I made some purchases.
Now I am going home to put up my wheat;
If it is Mohammed's will, I should have
A good harvest, since I planted a lot."
And the French responded, "You have spoken like a fool,   895
Since you believe Mohammed is God,
And that because of him you have bounty and riches,
Cold in winter and heat in summer.
We should cut off all your limbs!"
And William said, "Barons, let it be.   900
I would like to speak to him about something else."

34.
Count William began to speak to him, saying:
"Well, peasant, in the name of the faith by which you live,
Have you been in Nîmes, the fortified city?"
—"Indeed, sir, they even required me to pay a toll.   905
But since I am very poor, I could not pay it;
They let me pass because they noticed my children with me."
—"Tell me, peasant, about the city."
And he responded, "I can tell you about it.
We bought two big pieces of bread there for a penny.   910
The exchange rate there is double that of any other city.
Living there is not expensive unless things have become worse."
—"You fool," William said, "that is not what I am asking;
Rather, I want to know about the infidel knights,
And about King Otrant and his company."   915
The peasant answered, "I do not know anything about that
And would not want to lie about the subject."
The noble knight Garnier was there.
He was a vavasor and highly skilled in oratory,
And was a master of deceit.   920
He looked at the four oxen that they saw there.
"Sir," he said, "God bless me,
If someone had a thousand barrels similar
To the one on that wagon
And filled them with knights   925

And drove them on the route to Nîmes,
He would be able to take the city this way."
And William said, "By God, you're right.
I shall do it if my knights approve."

35.
On the advice Garnier gave,   930
They stopped the peasant in front of them
And gave him plenty to eat—
Bread, wine, claret, and spiced wine.
The peasant ate heartily,
And when he was satisfied,   935
Count William summoned his barons
And they came without delay.
When he saw them he began to speak:
"Barons," he said, "listen to me:
If someone were to take a thousand hooped barrels   940
Like the one you see on that wagon,
Fill them with armed knights,
And lead them along the stony route
Straight to Nîmes, the fortified city,
That person would be able to enter this way.   945
There would be no need to launch an assault."
And the knights responded, "You speak the truth,
Lord William, most noble one, it's worth thinking about.
There are definitely enough tumbrels in this land,
Plenty of wagons and carts.   950
Have your men return
By the route to Regordane that we passed
And take the oxen by force."
And William said, "That's an excellent idea."

36.
Following the advice Garnier had given them,   955
Count William had his men return
Fourteen long leagues to Regordane.
They took carts, oxen, and barrels.
The good peasants, who had made and assembled them,

Secured the barrels and the hitches.   960
Little did Bertrand care if the peasants complained.
Whoever spoke up was shamed,
Lost his eyes, and was hanged by the neck.

37.
If you had seen the uncouth peasants working so hard,
Carrying the adzes and axes,   965
Hooping the barrels and completely refinishing them,
Nailing up the wagons and carts,
And then watched the knights get into the barrels,
You would have been reminded of a great army.
They gave a big mallet to each knight   970
So that when they arrived in the city of Nîmes
And heard the head of the convoy blow the horn,
Our Frenchmen would be able to help.

38.
They put the lances in other barrels
On which they put two marks,   975
So that when they arrived among the savage race
The French soldiers would not be in danger.

39.
They put the shields in other barrels
On which they put two marks,
So that when they arrived among the Saracens,   980
The French would not be at a disadvantage.

40.
The count hurried to ready the convoy.
If you had seen the peasants of the region
Binding the barrels, fashioning and fitting them with lids,
And turning and balancing the wagons,   985
And the knights getting into the barrels,
You would have been reminded of a great army.
Now we must sing of Lord Bertrand
And how he was dressed.

He wore a tunic of dark woolen cloth   990
And a remarkable pair of shoes on his feet—
Large cowhide ones that were cracked on top.
"God," said Bertrand, "dear king of majesty,
These shoes will soon blister my feet!"
Hearing this, William burst out laughing.   995
"Nephew," said the count, "listen to me.
Lead these oxen down to the valley."
And Bertrand said, "You are wasting your breath.
I don't know how to prod or push them
Well enough to make them move."   1000
Hearing this, William burst out laughing.
But a bad thing happened to Bertrand
Because he knew nothing about driving oxen:
Before he realized it, his wagon hit mud
And sank up to the middle of the wheels.   1005
Seeing this, Bertrand nearly went out of his mind.
If you had seen him in the mud,
Raising the wheel with his shoulders,
You could have witnessed quite a spectacle!
His mouth and nose were bruised;   1010
Seeing this, William started to tease him:
"Dear nephew," he said, "listen to me.
You are involved in an activity now
About which you know absolutely nothing!"
Hearing this, Bertrand nearly went out of his mind.   1015
In the barrel that Bertrand was driving
Were the valiant knights Gilbert of Falaise,
Gautier of Termes, and Gilemer the Scot.
"Lord Bertrand, pay attention to how you drive,
We're scared of being turned upside down!"   1020
And Bertrand said, "That may soon happen!"
Now we must sing of those
Who had to drive the carts in the convoy.
They wore money sacks, pouches, belts,
And large purses to exchange money.   1025
They were riding on pitiful mules and packhorses.
If you had seen them traveling up the road,

You would think they were a wretched group!
In this realm, they could not travel
During the day without someone seeing them   1030
And taking them for merchants.
They passed the Gardon by a ford along the route
And camped on the other side in a meadow.
Now we must sing of William
And how he was dressed.   1035

41.
Count William wore a tunic
Of woolen cloth as was the custom in the region,
Large blue-green leggings on his legs,
And cowhide shoes that secured the leggings.
He had a belt that belonged to a local burgher,   1040
From which he hung a knife in a magnificent sheath;
And he rode a most pitiful mare.
He hung two old stirrups from his saddle
And his spurs were not new either;
They may have been thirty years old.   1045
He wore a felt hat on his head.

42.
Near the Gardon, along the banks,
They left two thousand armed men
From the company of William Fierebrace.
They kept the peasants away   1050
So that they would not spread the news
About what the French were going to pull from the barrels.
More than two thousand men prepared their goads;
They struck with their whips and started on their way.
Without stopping, they arrived at Necene,   1055
Then at Lavardi where the stone was quarried
For building the turrets of Nîmes.
The inhabitants of the city were going about their business
And began to discuss with each other what they saw:
"I see a lot of merchants arriving."   1060
—"You're right," said another, "I've never seen so many."

They followed the convoy closely until they came to the leader
And they asked him, "What are you carrying?"
—"Brocades, purple cloth, silk,
Expensive green and brown fabric,   1065
Sharp spears, hauberks, shiny helmets,
Heavy shields, and sharp swords."
The pagans said, "This is precious cargo.
Proceed now to the main marketplace."

43.
The French rode and traveled so swiftly,   1070
Crossing valleys, mountains, and hills,
That they arrived at the city of Nîmes.
They entered the gate with their carts
In single file, since the entrance was narrow.
News spread quickly throughout the land: 1075
"Rich merchants from another region
Are carrying goods unlike any ever brought here,
But they have sealed them all up in barrels."
King Otrant, who had heard this,
Came down the stairs with Harpin.   1080
They were brothers and loved each other very much,
And they were lords of the city.
They did not stop until they arrived at the market,
Accompanied by two hundred pagans.

44.
Listen, my lords, may God bless you,   1085
The glorious one, the son of holy Mary.
This song that I want to tell you
Is neither prideful nor foolish
Nor based on lies, but instead it recounts
The story of the brave men who conquered Spain   1090
And exalted Jesus and his religion.
This city of Nîmes, about which I am singing,
Is located in the land of my lord St. Giles.
In the city there was an ancient square
Where today the church of the Virgin is located;   1094a

At that time it did not exist, 1095
But was dedicated to the pagan religion
Where they prayed to Mohammed and his idols
And Tervagant in hopes that they would save them.
When the pagans held assembly and council,
They came from all over the city to meet there. 1100

45.
William came straightaway to a square
Where there was a green marble mounting block.
William Fierebrace dismounted there,
Took out his purse, unlaced the strings,
And removed a handful of coins. 1105
He asked who took care of collecting tolls
And added that he did not want the toll taker to do them any harm.
The pagans said, "You have nothing to fear.
There is not a man among us, no matter his lineage,
Who could say something harmful to you 1110
Without being hanged by the neck from a tree."

46.
As the pagans were speaking
To William in this manner,
Harpin and Otrant arrived
And asked to see the "famous" merchant. 1115
The pagans who were looking at William spoke up:
"He's right here, this worthy man
In the felt hat with the long beard;
He's the leader of the others."
King Otrant called him forward: 1120
"Where are you from, my dear merchant friend?"
—"Sir, we are from England,
From the great city of Canterbury."
—"Are you married, my dear merchant friend?"
—"Yes, to a very noble woman, and I have eighteen children, 1125
All of whom are young, except two who are grown.
One is named Begue and the other Sorant;
There they are, if you do not believe me."

And he pointed to Guielin and Bertrand,
His nephews, the sons of Bernard of Brabant.   1130
The pagans looked at them and said,
"Oh my, you have handsome children.
If only they knew how to dress properly!"
King Otrant spoke up:
"What's your name, my fair merchant friend?"   1135
—"My dear lord, I tell you truthfully, it's Tiacre."
The pagan responded, "That's a name belonging to a filthy race.
Brother Tiacre, what are you transporting?"
—"My lord, we are carrying brocades, taffetas, buckram,
Other fine purple and green fabrics,   1140
White hauberks, strong shiny helmets,
Sharp lances, good heavy shields,
And bright swords with shiny gold pommels."
Otrant responded, "Let's see, merchant."
And William said, "Lord, be patient,   1145
The most expensive merchandise is toward the back of the convoy."
—"What is toward the front, then?"
—"Ink, sulphur, incense, quicksilver,
Alum, grain, pepper, saffron,
Pelts, sheepskins, Cordovan leather,   1150
And marten furs, which are warm in the winter."
Otrant heard this and began to laugh heartily,
And the Saracens enjoyed it immensely.

47.
King Otrant spoke to him again,
"Brother Tiacre, by the faith you practice,   1155
Please tell us the truth.
In my opinion, you're carrying a lot of goods
In the convoy you're leading into the city.
Be so kind, please, to share some of them
With me and these other young men.   1160
You would profit from compensating us."
And William answered, "Fair lord, be patient,
I shall not leave the city today
Because it is beautiful and I would like to stay a while.

Before noon tomorrow,   1165
Before the call to vespers and before the sun sets,[7]
I shall give you plenty of my goods,
As much as the strongest among you can carry."
The pagans said, "Dear merchant, you are very valiant,
But you're generous only in word.   1170
We will see soon enough if you're truly a valiant man!"
—"Indeed," William replied, "and more than you know.
I have never been deceitful or stingy;
My goods are shared freely
With my close friends."   1175
The count asked one of his men,
"Tell me, have all my carts entered now?"
—"Yes indeed, my lord, thanks be to God."
He began to lead them through the streets.
Now you could see them moving freely in the vast squares,   1180
For William did not want to be trapped there,
But rather to be able to escape if the need arose.
William's men had blocked the door to the palace so well
That it would be difficult for the Saracens to enter it.

48.
King Otrant began to address him: 1185
"Brother Tiacre, in the name of the faith by which you live,
Where did you obtain such rich goods?
In which country and on which fief do you live?"
And William answered, "I can certainly tell you:
I acquired these goods in sweet France.   1190
Now, in fact, I am going to Lombardy,
To Calabria, to Apulia, to Sicily,
To Germany, then up to Romania,
To Tuscany, and from there to Hungary,
Then I shall return by way of Galicia,   1195
A rich region in Spain,
To Poitou, then up to Normandy,

---

7   It is rather curious that William mentions the call to vespers in Muslim territory. This is either
a slip or an indication of the jongleur's ignorance concerning Muslim religious practice.

To England and on to Scotland.
I shall not stop until I reach Wales.
I shall lead my men straight to Krak,   1200
To a very old fair there.
I shall trade in the kingdom of Venice."
The pagans added, "You have covered many countries;
No wonder you're so rich, peasant."

49.
Hear, my lords, in the name of the God of majesty,   1205
How William was recognized that day.
King Otrant looked at him
When William spoke in this manner
And he saw the bump on his nose.
At that moment, he remembered short-nosed William,   1210
The son of Aymeri of Narbonne by the Sea.
When he recognized him, he nearly lost his mind,
And his blood began to boil;
His heart sank and he almost fainted.
He spoke to him courteously   1215
In the manner you will now hear:
"Brother Tiacre, by the faith you practice,
That's a big bump you have on your nose.
Do tell me, who gave it to you?
Because I now remember short-nosed William,   1220
The greatly feared son of Aymeri,
Who killed members of my powerful family.
May it please Mohammed, my protector,
And Tervagant, and his holy graces
That I might hold him here in this city,   1225
As I hold you whom I see standing here.
In the name of Mohammed, he would soon be destroyed,
Hanged from the gallows and rocking in the wind,
Burned at the stake, or shamefully put to death!"
Hearing this, William burst out laughing.   1230
"My lord," he said, "listen to me.
Concerning what you just asked me,
I shall gladly and willingly tell you.

When I was a young boy, just an adolescent,
I became an amazing thief known for stealing 1235
And deceiving; I was the best.
I cut purses and well-secured money bags,
But I was caught by the young men
And merchants I had robbed.
They cut off my nose with their knives 1240
And left me to wander freely,
So I became the merchant you see before you.
Thanks to God, I acquired the many goods
That you see here today."
The pagan replied, "You are a valiant man. 1245
You should never be hanged from the gallows."
Then a Saracen left the scene;
Those who knew him called him Barré.
He was the seneschal of the king of the city;
He left to go prepare dinner 1250
And to light the fire in the kitchen.
He found the door of the palace
So blocked that he could not get in.
When he saw this, he nearly lost his mind
And swore by Mohammed that someone was going to regret it. 1255
He went to tell all this to Harpin,
Who was lord of the good city,
Along with his brother Otrant, the infidel.
He spoke to him most courteously:
"Noble lord, listen to me. 1260
By Mohammed, we have a real problem
Because of this peasant who arrived.
He has blocked the door of the palace so completely
That no one can get in or out.
If you believe me and follow my advice, 1265
Mark my words, we will anger and infuriate them.
Look at all these goods he has piled up here;
He doesn't want to give anything to you or to anyone else.
You should kill these oxen, my lord,
And have them taken to the kitchen to be prepared for dinner." 1270
And Harpin spoke, "Bring me a big mallet."

And the pagan answered, "Just as you wish."
The scoundrel left
And found an iron mallet
That he brought back and put in his hand.   1275
Harpin raised the mallet and killed Baillet,
Then Lovel who was next to him—
These were the two lead cart-oxen—
And had them skinned by the young man
In the kitchen in preparation for dinner.   1280
He thought he would satisfy his Saracens in this way,
But before they were able to enjoy a single morsel,
They would pay dearly, in my opinion,
Because one of the Frenchmen saw the whole thing.
And when he saw it, he was greatly disturbed   1285
And went to William to tell him everything that had happened.
He whispered in his ear in a low voice,
So that the Saracens and Slavs would not hear:
"By God, dear lord, a terrible thing has happened.
The pagans just killed two oxen from your convoy,   1290
The best two we brought with us
That belonged to the brave man you met,
The ones that were put at the front of the convoy.
Do you know who is hiding in the barrel on that cart?
The valiant Count Gilbert of Falaise by the Sea,   1295
Gautier of Termes, and Gilemer the Scot.
Your nephew, Bertrand, was responsible for them
And you did not protect them well."
Hearing this, William nearly went out of his mind;
He asked him quietly in a low voice,   1300
"Who did this? Tell me the truth."
—"By God, dear lord, you'll be sorry if you don't believe it.
It was Harpin, the villainous scoundrel."
—"Why the devil?" he asked them.
—"I don't know, dear lord, by the faith I have in God."   1305
When William heard this, he was furious,
But responded quietly in order not to be overheard:
"By St. Denis my protector,
They will pay dearly for this today!"

The Saracens gathered around him,   1310
Taunted him a lot, and tried to pick a quarrel with him.
King Harpin had ordered them to do this,
In hopes of starting a fight with William,
With the help of his brother, Otrant.

50.
Hear, my lords, may God bless you,   1315
How they tried to pick a quarrel with him.
King Otrant began to speak:
"Now then, peasant, may God curse you!
Why haven't you dressed your men
And yourself in fine fur-lined cloaks?   1320
You would be much better liked and respected."
And William responded, "That is of little value to me.
I would rather return,
Loaded down with riches,
To my wife who is waiting for me,   1325
Than furnish these men with new clothes."

51.
King Harpin responded angrily:
"Now then, peasant, may Mohammed bring harm upon you!
Why then do you wear big leather shoes
While your tunic and clothes are in such bad shape?   1330
You seem like a man who doesn't care how he looks."
He came up to William and yanked on his beard,
Pulling out almost a hundred hairs.
Seeing this, William nearly went out of his mind;
Then William grumbled without being heard: 1335
"Even though I'm wearing big leather shoes
And my clothes are in such bad shape,
I'm nonetheless called William Fierebrace,
The son of Aymeri of Narbonne, the wise one,
The noble and valorous count!   1340
This Saracen has insulted me,
He didn't recognize me when he pulled my beard.
By St. James the Apostle, he made a big mistake!"

52.

William spoke quietly as an aside:
"Even though my leggings are covered in mud   1345
And my tunic is too large and baggy,
Nonetheless my father is Lord Aymeri,
The one from Narbonne who has great courage.
I'm William, whose beard you pulled,
And, by St. Peter the Apostle, you made a big mistake   1350
That you will regret before this evening!"

53.

Hear, my lords—and may God cause you to prosper—
What William did next:
When he felt the hair pulled from his mustache
And heard that they had killed two oxen from his convoy,   1355
You can be sure that he was angry.
If he did not take vengeance he would go out of his mind!
William jumped on top of a mounting block
And began to shout with a clear voice:
"Treacherous pagans, may God destroy you!   1360
Today you have harassed and taunted me,
Calling me 'merchant' and 'peasant.'
Truthfully speaking, I'm not a peasant at all,
And my name is not Tiacre;
And, by the apostle they pray to in Nero's Meadow,   1365
You'll soon know what merchandise I'm carrying!
And you, Harpin, you arrogant scoundrel,
Why did you pull my beard and mustache?
You should know that it angered me immensely,
And I shall not eat again   1370
Until you have paid with your life."
William immediately rose up,
Grabbed him by the hair of his head with his left hand,
Pulled him toward him and leaned him forward,
Raised his big and strong right fist,   1375
And gave him such a blow
That it broke his jaw in two
And knocked him dead at his feet.

Seeing this, the pagans almost lost their minds
And started to shout with loud voices: 1380
"Thief, traitor, you will not escape!
In the name of Mohammed our protector,
Your body will experience great torture:
You'll be hanged or burnt, and your ashes scattered to the wind!
Woe to you for daring to touch King Harpin today."   1385
And then they immediately rushed at him.

54.
The pagans shouted, "Merchant, you're wrong!
Why did you kill King Harpin?
You'll regret it
And will never leave here alive!"   1390
There were many pagans with fists clenched before the duke;
They thought there were no more of our men.
Count William put a horn to his mouth
And blew it three times high and low.
When the knights who were hidden   1395
Within the barrels heard the signal,
They took mallets and knocked open the lids,
Then jumped out with swords drawn.
They shouted loudly, "Monjoie!"
There will soon be a heap of wounded and dead!   1400
As soon as the knights were out of the barrels,
They rushed out into the streets.

55.
The assault was fierce and vast,
And the ensuing battle harsh and horrible.
When the villainous traitors noticed   1405
That the French were fighting so fiercely,
They ran to get weapons, those villainous traitors!
The pagans armed themselves en masse
In their houses and living quarters;
They prepared to defend themselves   1410
And ran out of their lodgings with shield in hand.
At the sound of the horn, they gathered together.

There were a thousand valiant knights
In powerful William's troop;
Their fierce warhorses were brought to them   1415
And they immediately mounted.
They hung from their sides their heavy and sturdy shields
And held their sharp spears in their hands.
They rushed among the pagans,
Crying "Monjoie" in front and in back.   1420
The pagans fought for their lives,
And the city was crowded with people.
You would have seen there such a terrible battle,
So many lances splintering against heavy shields,
So many fine-meshed hauberks being broken,   1425
So many blood-covered Saracens falling dead!
No one escaped alive,
They all died there;
The ground was covered with blood.
Otrant turned around and ran.   1430

56.
The battle was fierce and harsh.
They struck many blows with their swords and spears.
Otrant fled because he feared death.
Count William followed him close at his back
And grabbed him by the mantle;   1435
Then he said to him two words in a loud voice:
"Do you know, Otrant, the kind of people I bring to justice?
It's this race that doesn't put their trust in God:
When I can capture them, they are dishonored.
Know for sure that your death is near!"   1440

57.
To this, proud-faced William added:
"Otrant, you evil king, may God curse you!
If you believe in the Son of Holy Mary,
Know for sure that your soul will be saved.
But if you don't believe in him, I swear to you   1445
That you'll lose your head,

All because of Mohammed who is worth nothing!"
And Otrant responded, "I don't know what to say about all this;
I shall follow my heart.
In the name of Mohammed, I completely refuse   1450
To believe in your God and renounce my own religion."
Hearing this, William nearly went out of his mind.
He dragged him down the stairs.
The French saw him and began to speak to him.

58.
The French shouted, "Otrant, speak the word   1455
That will postpone your death for six days!"
Count William shouted loudly,
"A hundred curses on whoever implores him further!"
Then they threw him out of one of the windows
And he was dead before he hit the ground.   1460
After him, they threw out a hundred more,
Whose arms and necks were broken instantly.

59.
Now the French have liberated the city,
The high towers and the paved rooms.
They found there much wine and wheat;   1465
The city would not suffer famine for seven years,
Nor be conquered, nor harmed.
It bothered William that the French did not know about the victory,
That is to say, the thousand knights who had remained in camp.
Someone blew a horn in the palace   1470
So that those who remained outside the walls heard.
They mounted their horses right away
And did not stop until they arrived in Nîmes.
When they arrived, they expressed great joy,
As did the peasants who were following them,   1475
And who asked for their carts and oxen to be returned.
The French were happy and did not withhold anything:
The peasants did not lose a single penny
That was not generously returned to them.
They in fact ended up with a surplus.   1480

The peasants returned to their country.
The news spread throughout France:
Count William had liberated Nîmes.
News was sent to Louis,
Who was very happy when he heard it.   1485
He praised God, and Mary his mother.

3

The Conquest of Orange

1.

Listen, my lords—and may glorious God,
Son of holy Mary, grant you his blessing—
To a good song that I wish to tell you!
It is not about pride or folly,
Nor is it derived or drawn from false tales,   5
But it tells of the brave men who conquered Spain.
Those who go to Saint-Gilles know it well;
They have seen the proof in Brioude:
They have seen William's shield and his rosette-adorned buckler,
And the shield of Bertrand, his noble nephew.[1]   10
I do not think any cleric would contradict me,
Nor would any writing found in a book.
Everyone has sung of the city of Nîmes:
William has it in his possession,
Its high walls and halls of stone,   15
And its palaces and fortifications;
But, by God, he doesn't yet hold Orange!
Few are the men who speak truly about this,
But I will tell the truth, for I learned it long ago,

---

1   Pilgrims taking the Regordane Way to Saint-Gilles, an important stop on one of the pilgrimage routes to Santiago de Compostela, stopped at the abbey-church in Brioude to visit St. Julian's tomb. In the *Moniage Guillaume*, William temporarily retreats from the military life and deposits his shield on the altar of the church in Brioude.

About the way Orange was crushed and ravaged;   20
This was accomplished by proud-faced William,
Who expelled from Orange the pagans of Almeria,
And those from Susce and those from Pincernie,
Those from Baghdad and those from Tabarie.
He took Queen Orable as his wife;   25
She had been born of the pagan race
And was once the wife of King Tibaut of Africa,
But she came to believe in God, son of holy Mary,
And established churches and abbeys.
Few are those who can tell you this tale.   30

2.
Listen, my lords, noble and honest knights!
Would it please you to hear a song of great exploits,
How Count William stormed Orange?
He took as his wife wise Lady Orable;
She had been married to King Tibaut of Persia.   35
Before gaining her love
William truly suffered many hardships;
Many days he fasted and kept vigil many nights.

3.
It was in May, in the springtime;[2]
The woods were blossoming and the meadows turning green,   40
The gentle rivers were returning to their channels,
The birds were singing sweetly and pleasantly.
Count William arose early in the morning;
He went to church to hear the service,
Then left when it had finished   45
And went up to the palace of the infidel Otrant,
Which he had conquered with formidable audacity.
He leaned upon the sills of the great windows;
He gazed out at the country below him,

---

2   As in *The Convoy to Nîmes*, lines 13–16, *The Conquest of Orange* adopts the springtime beginning
or *reverdie* found in medieval love lyric and romance. Here the motif serves to foreshadow William's
pursuit of Queen Orable.

Saw the fresh grass and the rose gardens,   50
And heard the thrush and the blackbird singing.
He then remembered the life of pleasure
He used to lead in France.
He called Bertrand, "Lord nephew, come here.
We left France as very poor men,   55
Without bringing harpists or minstrels
Or maidens to entertain us.
We have plenty of good swift horses
And solid hauberks and fine gilded helms,
Sharp swords and fine shields with bosses,   60
And solid lances with stout blades,
And bread and wine and cured meats and grain.
And may God destroy the Saracens and Slavs
Who allow us to sleep and rest for so long,
Since they have not crossed the sea with their forces   65
So that we could all prove ourselves.
It grieves me to stay here doing nothing!
We are confined here just like
A man in prison."
William has complained most foolishly: 70
Before the sun sets and evening falls,
He will hear news
That will make him quite angry and irate.

4.
Thus William stood at the windows in the open air,
In the company of sixty Frenchmen,   75
All wearing fresh white ermine,
Silken breeches, and shoes of Cordovan leather;
Most held their young falcons ready to fly.
Count William's heart was filled with joy;
He looked down toward a steep ravine,   80
Saw the green grass, the flowering rosebush,
And heard the oriole and the blackbird in song.
He called out to Guielin and Bertrand,
His two beloved nephews:
"Listen to me, noble and valiant knights.   85

We left France just a short time ago;
If we now had a thousand maidens here with us,
Frenchwomen with charming, graceful bodies,
And if these barons could be entertained by them,
And I too could be courting them,   90
I would be most delighted.
We have plenty of fine, swift horses
And solid hauberks and fine gleaming helms,
Sharp lances and good heavy shields,
Fine swords with silver hilts,   95
And bread and wine, cured meats and grain.
May God destroy the Saracens and Persians
Who fail to cross the sea in full force!
Staying here now bores me to no end,
For I have no chance to prove my bravery."   100
He was complaining most foolishly:
Before the setting sun and the fall of evening,
He would hear momentous news
That would make him angry and sorrowful.

5.
Thus William stood at the windows in the wall   105
With more than a hundred Frenchmen,
All clothed in fine ermine.
He looked down at the roaring Rhône River
That ran along the road coming from the east,
And he saw an escaped prisoner emerge from the water.   110
It was Gilbert, from the city of Lenu.
He had been captured on the Rhône, on a bridge,
    in a noisy surprise attack.
The Turks had taken him to Orange;
For three years they had kept and held him,
Until one morning, at daybreak,   115
When it pleased God to let him escape.
A Saracen untied him of his own accord
And then insulted and beat him brutally.
The valiant knight was sorely grieved, for he had
    been imprisoned so long;

He seized the Saracen by a tuft of his hair, pulling him down,   120
And dealt him such a blow on the neck with his strong fist
That he shattered both his spine and his torso,
Knocking him dead at his feet.
He lowered himself out of the window;
He would not be seized or held captive again.   125
He went all the way to Nîmes without stopping;
That very day he would bring such tidings
To our barons, who were talking of revelry,
That would cause William trouble,
Rather than bring him pleasure with naked women.   130

6.
Thus valiant William stood at the window.
The escaped prisoner had crossed the Rhône;
He climbed the hills and descended into the valleys,
Never stopping until he reached Nîmes.
He entered by the gate of the fair city   135
And found William beneath the thick branches of a pine tree,
Accompanied by many a renowned knight.
Beneath the pine tree a minstrel was singing
An old and very ancient song;
It was a fine song that pleased the count.   140
Gilbert came up the stairs;
Seeing him, William began to examine him
And saw that he was filthy, pallid, discolored,
Thin and pale, shaggy and gaunt.
He thought he must be a Saracen or a Slav   145
Who had made his way across the sea
To announce his news and have it heard;
But then the escaped prisoner greeted him:
"May the Lord God, who made wine and grain,
And gives us light and brightness from the heavens,   150
And makes men and women walk and speak,
Preserve William, the short-nosed marquis,
The flower of France, and his noble knights,
The warriors I see gathered here!"
—"My good friend and brother, may God bless you!   155

But tell us now, and do not hide anything:
Who told you my name was William?"
—"My lord," he said, "you will hear the truth:
It was in Orange, where I was held for a long time;
I could never manage to escape,   160
Until one morning at daybreak
When it was the will of Jesus that I be set free."
And William said, "May God be praised!
But tell me now, and do not hide anything:
What is your name and where were you born?"   165
—"My lord," he said, "you will hear the truth;
But I am completely worn out and exhausted
From staying awake by night and fasting by day;
I have not eaten for four whole days."
And William replied, "You will have plenty."   170
The count summoned his chamberlain:
"Bring him a plentiful meal
With bread and wine and spiced drinks and aromatic liqueurs,
Cranes and geese and peacocks in pepper sauce."
And he did all that his lord commanded.   175
When Gilbert had eaten his fill,
He willingly sat at the count's feet
And began to tell his tale.

7.
William saw the unfamiliar messenger,
And called to him, asking: 180
"Where were you born, my friend, and in what country?
What is your name and where in France do you live?"
Gilbert, a most valiant man, replied:
"I am the son of Guy, the duke who held the Ardennes;
He held Artois and Vermandois in his power.   185
I was coming from Germany by way of Burgundy,
And I set sail on Lake Geneva in Lausanne.
A strong wind and violent storm took me by surprise
And brought me to the port of Geneva.
Pagans captured me in Lyon on the Rhône River   190
And took me to the port of Orange.

There is no such fortress from here to the River Jordan!
The walls are high and the tower tall and wide,
As are the palace and adjoining structures.
Inside are twenty thousand pagans armed with lances,   195
And seven score Turks with colorful banners,
All of whom carefully guard the city of Orange,
For they greatly fear that Louis might capture it—
And you too, my lord, and the barons of France.
Also there is Aragon, a powerful Saracen king,   200
Son of Tibaut from the kingdom of Spain,
And Lady Orable, a gracious queen:
There is none so beautiful from here to the Orient.
She has a lovely body, slender and elegant,
Skin as white as a flower on a tree.   205
God! Her beauty and youth are in vain
Since she does not believe in God, the omnipotent Father!"
—"Truly," said William, "such great power!
But, in the name of him in whom I trust,
I no longer wish to bear shield or lance   210
Unless I bear my banner there."

8.
Count William listened to the baron;
He sat down beside him on a large block of stone
And spoke to him amiably, saying:
"Fair friend and brother, you have spoken well.   215
Did the Saracens ever keep you in prison?"
—"Yes, truly, my lord, three years and fifteen days,
And I was unable to fight my way out
Until God granted one morning
That a treacherous and insolent Saracen   220
Wanted to beat me as he did each day.
I grabbed him by a tuft of hair on his forehead
And dealt him such a blow to the neck with my fist
That I completely shattered his neck bone.
I escaped alone through the window,   225
Without being noticed by any of the Saracens.
I came to Beaucaire, the port at Oriflor,

Where I found
Turks and Persians, and King Aragon,
The eldest son of Tibaut the Slav.   230
He is large and burly, powerful and tall;
His head is wide and his forehead low;
His fingernails are long and pointed.
There is no tyrant like him under God's heaven!
He slays and destroys our Christian brethren.   235
If someone were to take the city and the tower
And kill this wicked traitor,
His labor would be well spent."

9.
"Fair friend and brother," said valiant William,
"Is Orange really as you have described it?"   240
Gilbert replied, "It is even better!
If only you could see the main palace,
How tall it is, and fortified all around!
From top to bottom there are many things to behold.
If you were there on the first day of summer,   245
You would hear the little birds singing,
Falcons and molted goshawks shrieking,
Horses whinnying and mules braying,
Saracens enjoying and amusing themselves,
Sweet-smelling herbs,   250
And chrysanthemums and cinnamon in abundance.
There you could gaze upon Lady Orable,
The wife of King Tibaut the Slav;
There is no greater beauty to be found in all of Christendom,
Nor in any pagan land: 255
She has a lovely body, slender and shapely,
And sparkling eyes like those of a molted falcon.
What a shame that her great beauty is in vain,
Since she believes neither in God nor in his goodness!
A noble man could take great pleasure in her company,   260
And she could be saved if she loved God."
And William replied, "By the faith I owe St. Omer,
Fair friend and brother, you praise her well;

By the all-saving one,
I no longer wish to bear lance or shield   265
Unless I conquer the lady and the city."

10.
"My friend, fair brother, is Orange really so magnificent?"
The escaped prisoner replied, "God help me, fair lord,
If only you could see the palace in that city,
With its vaults and marble floors!   270
It was built by Griffon of Almeria,
A highly skilled and cunning Saracen;
There is no flower from here to pagan lands
That is not masterfully painted there in gold.
Inside lives Queen Orable,   275
The wife of King Tibaut of Africa;
There is no greater beauty in all of pagandom:
She has a lovely neck, and she is slender and slim.
Her skin is as white as the hawthorn blossom;
Her eyes are clear and sparkling, ever laughing.   280
What a shame that her beauty is in vain,
Since she does not believe in God, son of holy Mary!"
—"Truly," said William, "you have praised her highly,
But by the faith I owe my beloved,
I shall eat no bread made with flour,   285
Or cured meat, and I shall drink no aged wine,
Until I have seen how Orange is laid out!
I shall also see the marble tower
And Lady Orable, the courtly queen;
The love I feel for her torments and dominates me[3]   290
More than I could ever imagine or describe.
If I cannot have her, I shall soon lose my life."
—"That is pure folly," the escaped prisoner replied,
"If you were now in the palace of that city,
And if you could see the Saracens,   295
May God destroy me if you had any hope of living long enough

---

3   The motif of *amor de lonh* (love from a distance, by hearsay) is a staple of courtly lyric and
romance.

To emerge from that place by nightfall in one piece!
Forget all of this, it is madness."

11.
William heard the anxious words
Spoken and uttered by the escaped prisoner;   300
He summoned his countrymen:
"I seek your advice, noble and honorable knights;
This escaped prisoner has praised the city of Orange;
I have never been there and do not know the region.
The swift-moving Rhône River flows there;   305
If not for that, I would have sowed panic in that city."
The escaped prisoner said, "That is pure folly!
If there were a hundred thousand of you armed with swords,
With splendid armor and golden shields,
Attempting to engage battle,   310
And even if there were no river or obstacle of any kind,
Before you entered by the great gates
A thousand sword-blows would be dealt,
And so many saddle girths broken, and so many shields pierced,
And so many barons struck down on the road!   315
Forget all of this, it is madness."

12.
"Truly," said William, "this is most alarming!
You have just told me that no count or king
Has such a city in his possession,
And yet you reproach me for wanting to go there!   320
By St. Maurice to whom they pray in the Amienois,
I bid you to come with me;
But we shall bring neither warhorse nor palfrey,
Nor shining armor, nor helms from the Amienois,
Nor shield, nor lance, nor spear from Poitou,   325
But rather hooded capes to disguise us as poor pilgrims.
When you were in the region, you spoke a good bit of Turkish,
As well as African, Bedouin, and Basque."
You can imagine how distressed the escaped prisoner was to hear
    this!

He would rather have been in Chartres or Blois   330
Or Paris, in the king's lands:
Now he has no idea how to get out of this predicament.

13.
Now William was angry and irate;
His nephew Bertrand spoke to him in this way:
"Uncle," he said, "give up this foolish idea.   335
If you were now in the palace in that city,
And if you encountered the Saracens,
They would recognize you by the bump on your nose
    and by your laughter,
And they would know instantly that you were a spy.
And then, perhaps, they would take you away to Persia,   340
Where they would eat you without bread or flour.[4]
They would not waste any time before killing you,
Or they would throw you into a stone prison,
Where you would remain your entire life
Until King Tibaut of Africa would arrive,   345
Along with Desramé and Goliath of Bile,
Who would condemn you to death.
If you were put to death because of love,
Then your people would say
That it was an ill-fated day when you set eyes upon Queen
    Orable."   350
—"Truly," replied William, "I have no fear of that,
For, by the apostle to whom they pray in Galicia,
I would rather perish and lose my life
Than eat bread made with flour
Or cured meat, or drink well-aged wine,   355
Before I see how Orange is laid out,
And Gloriette, the marble tower,
And Lady Orable, the courtly queen!
The love I feel for her torments and dominates me;
A man in love is seized with madness."   360

---

4   Saracens were not infrequently accused of cannibalism in the chansons de geste. See Régnier
314n341.

14.

Thus William was unnerved because of Orange;
His nephew Bertrand began to admonish him:
"Uncle," he said, "you want to disgrace yourself
And cover yourself with shame, and have your limbs cut off!"
—"Truly," replied the count, "I am not afraid of that;   365
A man in love is completely mad.
Nothing will stop me—even if I were torn limb from limb,
Or if someone were to beg me—
From going to see how Orange is laid out,
And Lady Orable, so worthy of praise.   370
The love I feel for her has so dominated me
That I cannot sleep or rest at night;
Nor can I eat or drink
Or mount my warhorse
Or go to mass or even enter a church."   375
The baron had black powder ground in a mortar
Along with other herbs he knew well.
With the help of Gilbert, who dared not leave him,
They painted their bodies front and back,
Their faces, chests, and feet;   380
They perfectly resembled devils and demons.
Guielin said, "By St. Riquier,
It is amazing how the two of you are transformed:
Now you can travel the whole world
Without being recognized by a living soul.   385
But, by the apostle they seek in Rome,
Nothing will stop me, even if I were torn limb from limb,
From going with you to see how it all turns out!"
He rubbed on the ointment and painted himself;
Now all three of them were perfectly ready!   390
They departed the city, taking their leave.
"God," said Bertrand, "dear righteous Father,
How we are now tricked and betrayed!
What folly sparked this enterprise
That will cause us nothing but shame and disgrace,   395
If God, who judges all things, does not attend to it!"

15.

William, the proud-faced marquis, took his leave
With Gilbert and the proud Guielin.
Count Bertrand turned back,
While the others proceeded without delay.   400
Below Beaucaire they came upon the Rhône
And crossed it with great precaution,
Rowing quietly.
Then they passed the Sorgue without barge or boat,
And passing Avignon, they continued   405
Directly to Orange, to its walls and moats,
Its high halls and its palace adorned with mosaics,
Its ornamental balls and golden eagles.
They heard fledgling birds singing inside,
Falcons and molted goshawks crying,   410
Horses neighing and mules braying,
And Saracens amusing themselves in the tower.
The air was filled with the pleasing scent
    of chrysanthemums and cinnamon,
And an abundance of sweet-smelling herbs.
"God," said William, "who gave me life,   415
What a magnificent city!
Whoever governs it is rich and powerful!"
They went up to the city gate without delay.
Gilbert called to the gatekeeper,
Speaking to him courteously in his language: 420
"Open up, gatekeeper, let us in;
We are interpreters from Africa and across the sea,
And we are vassals of King Tibaut the Slav."
The gatekeeper replied, "I have never heard such a thing!
Who are you people calling to me from outside?   425
King Aragon has not yet risen from his bed,
And I dare not open the gate,
For we greatly fear short-nosed William
Who captured Nîmes with formidable audacity.
Stay there, while I go and tell the king;   430
If he so commands it, I shall let you enter."
—"Go at once, then," said valiant William,

"Go quickly and don't wait!"
The gatekeeper left without delay;
He climbed the marble steps of the palace   435
And found Aragon seated beside a pillar,
Surrounded by Saracens and Slavs.
He addressed the king courteously, saying:
"My lord, listen to me:
Three honorable Turks are at the city gate,   440
Saying that they come from Africa, from across the sea."
—"Go then, fair friend, and let them enter;
I wish to ask them for news
Of my father, whose arrival is long overdue."
The gatekeeper hurried to open the gate for them.   445
Thus William entered the city of Orange
With Gilbert and the valiant Guielin;
But they will not leave as soon as they might wish:
They will first suffer much pain and hardship.

16.
Now William was inside the city of Orange   450
With Guielin and the noble Gilbert.
They were heavily made up with alum and ink.
They greatly resembled Saracens or pagans.
In the palace, they came upon two Saracens
Absorbed in conversation.   455
One said to the other, "Those men came from Africa;
Today we will hear some good news."
Count William made his way
To the palace of King Tibaut the Persian.
The pillars and the walls between them were marble,   460
The windows inlaid with silver,
And the golden eagle shining and gleaming.
There was neither ray of sunshine nor breath of wind.
"God," said William, "dear Father, heavenly king,
Who has ever seen such a beautiful palace?   465
Its lord is tremendously rich and powerful!
If only it pleased God, who created all humanity,
That the paladin Bertrand were here

With ten thousand fighting Frenchmen!
Today would then mark the beginning of a bad year for the
    Saracens;   470
I myself would kill more than a hundred of them before noon."
He found Aragon sitting beside a pillar,
Surrounded by fifteen thousand Persians.
William is a dead man if he does not lie through his teeth.
Now you will hear what he said to them: 475
"Emir, my lord, noble and valiant knight,
May Mohammed and the god Tervagant preserve you!"
The emir said, "Barons, come forward.
Where do you come from?"—"From the African kingdom
Of your father, the mighty king Tibaut.   480
Yesterday morning as the bells were sounding for morning
    prayers,
We were in the fine, strong city of Nîmes.
We hoped to find the powerful king Otrant
And Synagon and Harpin the tyrant.
But William, along with the French barons, killed him.   485
They massacred our men, slashed them to pieces.
William imprisoned all three of us,
But he has so many friends and kinsmen
That he let us leave for some reason;
I do not know why, but may the devil take him!"   490
—"I find this most distressing," Aragon said,
"By Mohammed, in whom I believe,
If I had William here in this city,
He would be tortured and killed at once!
I would scatter his bones and ashes to the wind."   495
Hearing this, William bowed his head;
He would rather have been in Paris or Sens.
He fervently implored God the Father:
"Glorious Lord, who created all humanity,
You who were born of the Virgin in Bethlehem   500
When the three kings came searching for you;
You suffered on the cross at the hands of cruel men,
And you were struck by a lance in your side—
The blind Longinus did this,

Such that blood and water flowed onto his hands;   505
He rubbed his eyes and recovered his sight.
As surely as I speak the truth,
Protect us from death and torture;
Let us not be slain by Saracens and Persians."

17.
Now William was in the palace at the foot of the tower.   510
He called to his companions
In a low voice, because of the pagans:
"My lords," he said, "we shall be imprisoned
If God by his most holy name does not watch over us!"
—"Uncle William," replied Guielin,   515
"My noble lord, you came here seeking love.
Behold Gloriette, the palace and the tower:
Ask where the ladies are!
You can easily play the fool."
The count replied, "You are right, young man."   520
King Aragon spoke to him in this way:
"When were you in Africa, valiant knights?"
—"My dear lord, no more than two months ago."
—"Did you see King Tibaut of Aragon?"
—"Yes, fair lord, at the citadel of Vaudon.   525
He kissed us and sent us to ask you
To protect his city and his lands.
Where is his wife? Will you let us see her?"
—"Yes, my lords," replied King Aragon,
"There is not a more beautiful woman from here to the clouds.   530
Barons," he said, "I need my father here:
The French are seizing our palaces and our towers;
It is William who has done this, along with his two nephews;
But by the faith that I owe Tervagant and Mohammed,
If I held William as my prisoner,   535
He would soon be burned in a fire or on hot coals,
And I would cast his bones and ashes to the winds!"
Hearing this, William bowed his head;
At that moment he would rather have been in Reims or Laon.
He invoked God and His glorious name: 540

"God of glory, you who created Lazarus
And became incarnate in the Virgin,
Protect me from death and imprisonment,
So that these vicious Saracens do not kill us."

18.
Now William was inside the splendid palace.   545
The pagans and Saracens called for water;
The tables were set, and they sat down to eat.
William sat at the table with his nephew Guielin;
They spoke softly, keeping their heads lowered,
Greatly fearing that they might be captured.   550
King Aragon had them served quite well:
They had abundant bread and wine,
Cranes and wild goose and excellent roast peacock.
I know not what to tell you about the other dishes,
Except that there was as much as they could desire.   555
When they had eaten and drunk their fill,
The stewards removed the tablecloths.
The pagans and Saracens played chess.
William listened to the sounds of the palace,
Which was inlaid with green and gray-brown marble.   560
He saw the birds and painted lions.
"God," said the count, "you who were hung on the cross,
Who has ever seen a more exquisite palace?
If only it pleased God, who has never lied,
That Bertrand the paladin were here   565
With twenty thousand Frenchmen clad in armor!
Before the end of the day the pagans would come to a bitter end.
By my head, I myself would kill four score of them!"

19.
King Aragon called to William
And had him sit beside him next to a pillar;   570
He whispered softly in his ear:
"Noble Turk," he said, "now tell me the truth:
What sort of man is this short-nosed William
Who captured Nîmes with formidable audacity

And killed King Harpin and his brother? 575
Has he already thrown you into his prison?"
And William replied, "You shall hear the truth.
He is so powerful, rich, and wealthy
That he cares nothing for fine gold and shining silver;
Instead he set us free for nothing, 580
But he did make us swear upon our religion—
We cannot hide this from you—to order you
To escape across the sea to Africa.
Before you see the end of May,
He will follow you with twenty thousand armed soldiers. 585
Towers and pillars will not protect you,
Nor will vast halls or deep ditches:
They will be pierced and shattered by iron clubs.
If he captures you, you will be tortured
And hanged on the gallows, swaying with the wind." 590
Aragon replied, "That is pure madness!
I myself will send a message to Africa across the sea.
My father will come with his powerful barons,
Goliath and King Desramé,
Corsolt of Mables and his brother Aceré, 595
And Clareau and King Atriblé
And Quinzepaumes and King Sorgalé,
The King of Egypt and King Codroé,
And King Morant and King Anublé,
And the Saracen chief of Sorgremont by the Sea, 600
My uncle Bourreau and his sons, armed to the teeth,
The thirty kings born in Spain.
Each will bring twenty thousand armed soldiers,
And we shall attack them at the walls and moats.
William will perish and lose his life, 605
And his nephews will hang from the gallows."
Hearing this, William thought he would lose his mind.
Under his breath he replied softly:
"By God," he said, "foul wretch, you are quite mistaken!
Rather, three thousand Turks will be killed 610
Before you ever become prince of Nîmes or hold it in fief."
If he had been equipped with weapons,

The entire palace would already have been terrified,
For reason could never have calmed his temper.

20.

Now William was in the great stone hall.   615
"King Aragon," he began,
"Lord," he said, "show me the queen
Whom the emperor of Africa loves so much."
—"The emperor acts most foolishly," Aragon replied,
"For he is old, with a white beard,   620
And she is a young and beautiful woman:
There is none more beautiful in all of pagandom.
In Gloriette she carries on her love affairs;
She would prefer to have Sorbant of Venice,
A young man with a newly grown beard   625
Who knows a thing or two about arms and pleasure,
Rather than Tibaut of Esclavonia.
An old man who loves a young woman is a great fool:
He is soon cuckolded and ridiculed."
Hearing this, William began to laugh: 630
"Truly," said William, "you have no use for her, then?"
—"Not I, certainly, may the Lord God curse her!
I wish she were in Africa
Or in Baghdad, in the realm of Almeria."

21.

Noble William left the palace[5]   635
Along with Gilbert and the mighty Guielin.
They crossed the great hall;
A pagan, Malcuidant, led them
To the queen, whom the king loved so much.
They would have been better off returning   640
To the other side of the Rhône, toward the great city of Nîmes.
Before nightfall or sunset,

---

5   The word "palace" designates several places in the text: the royal palace occupied by Tibaut
and Aragon, the great hall of Tibaut's palace, and Gloriette, the tower or palace serving as Orable's
residence.

If God does not watch over them by his holy command,
They will hear news that will make them unhappy.
Then they entered Gloriette.   645
The pillars and walls in between were of marble,
And the windows inlaid with silver;
And the golden eagle gleamed and shone.
There was neither ray of sunshine nor breath of wind;
The tower was beautifully decorated, and very pleasing.   650
On one side of the interior chamber
There was a pine tree with magical properties
That you will hear about, if you wish.
Long are its branches and its foliage abundant;
The flower it bears is magnificent—   655
White, blue, and crimson.
There, conversations were often held.
Chrysanthemums, cinnamon, galangal, and incense
Exhale sweet fragrances, along with hyssop and lemon balm.
There sat Orable, Tibaut of Africant's wife.   660
She was dressed in a gown of Persian silk,
The sides tightly laced up her beautiful body
With rich silk cord.
And Rosiane, niece of Rubiant,
Fanned her with a silver fan.   665
She was whiter than glistening snow
And more crimson than a fragrant rose.
When William saw her, his blood stirred.
He greeted her handsomely and courteously:
"May the God we believe in preserve you!"   670
The queen said, "Baron, come forward.
May God, to whom the world belongs, preserve you."
She seated them beside her on a bench
That was inlaid with gold and silver.
Now they could speak as they wished.   675
"God," said William, "this is paradise!"
Guielin said, "I have never seen such a fine place.
I wish I could spend my entire life here;
I would never want to leave it for any reason."

22.

Now William was seated in Gloriette   680
With Gilbert and brave Guielin,
Beside the maidens beneath the shade of the pine tree.
There sat Orable, the fair-faced lady;
She was clad in an ermine-lined cloak
And, beneath, a silken tunic,   685
Tightly laced up her lovely body.
When William saw her, his whole body trembled.
"God," said William, "this is paradise!"
—"So help me God," replied Guielin,
"I would willingly stay here forever;   690
I would no longer wish to eat or sleep!"
The noble lady spoke to them thus:
"Where are you from, worthy and noble knights?"
—"My lady, we are from the kingdom of Persia,
The land of your husband Tibaut.   695
Yesterday morning at daybreak
We were in Nîmes, that splendid city.
We were hoping to find men of our lineage—
King Synagon and Otrant and Harpin—
But William Fierebrace had killed all three.   700
The French captured us at the city gates
And brought us before the paladin.
But he is so powerful and surrounded by allies
That he cares nothing for silver or fine gold;
Rather, he allowed us to escape with this stipulation: 705
We had to swear upon our religion
To deliver his order
That you flee to the kingdom of Persia;
For before you see the end of April
He will pursue you with twenty thousand soldiers clad in armor;   710
Neither walls nor palisades will protect you,
Nor great halls nor wooden fortifications;
With iron mauls these will all be destroyed.
If he can capture Aragon the Arab,
Your stepson, whom you love so much,   715
He will have him suffer a horrible death,

By hanging or burning and roasting in flames."
Hearing this, the lady sighed.

23.
The lady listened to the foreign messengers;
Then she addressed them without delay: 720
"My lords, worthy barons, I understand what you are saying.
What kind of man, then, is this William Fierebrace
Who captured Nîmes, the palace and the great halls,
Who killed my men and who still threatens me?"
—"Truly," said the count, "he is quite proud-tempered;   725
He has powerful fists and amazing arms.
There is no man from here to Arabia, no matter how large,
Who, if struck by William's sharp sword,
Would not have his body and armor sliced through:
That sharp sword swings all the way down to the ground."   730
—"Truly," said the lady, "this is most distressing.
By Mohammed, he must govern his land well;
Happy is the lady who has his heart!"
Wicked pagans were arriving in throngs.
Before the day was out, William would hear dreadful things   735
Such as he had never heard in his entire life.
May God preserve him from death and misfortune!

24.
Now William was up in the tower
With Guielin and valiant Gilbert,
Beside the maidens under the thick branches of the pine tree;   740
He spoke softly to the queen.
Wicked pagans had gathered there
To watch and observe the barons.
If God, who suffered on the cross, does not watch over them,
William will be ill-treated today.   745
Now behold a pagan, Salatré;
May he be confounded by the one who saves all things!
The count captured him in the city of Nîmes;
One evening the foul wretch escaped,
Fleeing the entire length of a ditch   750

So that he could not be caught or found.
He hatched an evil plot against William,
As you will hear presently.
He came and sat beside Aragon;
Speaking softly in his ear, he said,   755
"By Mohammed, my lord, here is a chance to increase your glory;
Soon they will be repaid for the harsh cruelty
They wanted to inflict on me in the city of Nîmes.
Now, do you see that strong, arrogant man?
That is William, the short-nosed marquis;   760
And the other young man is his nephew;
And the third one, holding the heavy club,
Is the marquis who escaped from here.
They have disguised themselves to betray you,
And they plan to take this good city."   765
—"Are you telling me the truth?" asked Aragon.
—"My lord," he said, "woe unto you if you do not believe me.
See William over there: he threw me in prison
And would have hanged me and let me swing in the wind,
If Mohammed had not protected me.   770
Today he will get what he deserves!"
Now hear, valiant and noble barons,
For the love of God, who suffered on the cross,
How the scoundrel went to work:
He took a goblet of wine and hurled it at William.   775
The goblet was made entirely of fine, pure gold,
And it struck William on the forehead above his nose;
William's makeup faded and his true skin color appeared:
His skin was as white as a summer flower.
Seeing this, William thought he would lose his mind.   780
All the blood in his body froze;
He called upon God, the king of majesty:
"Glorious Father, who saves all things
And who deigned to become flesh in the Virgin;
Because you wished to save the people of this world,   785
You allowed yourself to suffer great torment
And be struck and wounded on the cross.
As surely as this is true, by your goodness,

Preserve me from death and evil:
Don't let us be killed by Saracens and Slavs!" 790

25.
When Aragon heard the Slav say
That he recognized all three companions,
He leapt to his feet and spoke to them:
"Lord William, we know your name well.
Ill-fated was the hour you crossed the Rhône, by Mohammed! 795
You will all die a horrible death:
We will scatter your bones and ashes to the wind.
I would not accept all the gold kept in this castle
To spare you from dying and being reduced to ashes."
Hearing this, William turned red as a flaming coal; 800
He would rather have been in Reims or Laon.
Guielin saw that they had nowhere to hide;
He wrung his hands and tore out his hair.
"God," said William, "by your most holy name,
Glorious Father, who created Lazarus 805
And became flesh in the Virgin,
Who rescued Jonah from the belly of the whale
And Daniel from the lion's den;
Who pardoned Mary Magdalene,
And placed St. Peter's relics in Nero's Meadow; 810
Who converted St. Paul, his companion,
Who was at the time a most cruel man,
But he became one of the believers,
And followed along with the others.
As surely as this is true, Lord, and we believe it, 815
Preserve us from death and imprisonment:
Do not let us be killed by these treacherous Saracens!"
He had a staff, large, sturdy, and long;
With two hands he raised it high
And struck Salatré, the foul wretch 820
Who had denounced him to Aragon;
Right in the middle of the head, he struck him hard with the staff
So that his brains came flying out.
"Monjoie!" he cried, "Barons, attack!"

26.

William struck terror into the palace;   825
He killed the pagan right in front of the king.
Count William then noticed a log
That had been brought in to build a fire.
He made his way to it at full speed, sweating profusely;
He grabbed it in his fists and raised it high;   830
He struck the vicious Baitaime
Right in the middle of his head, with a fierce blow of the club,
Which made his brains fly out of his head;
In front of the king he struck him dead.
And Gilbert went to strike Quarré,   835
Ramming a pole into his stomach
So that a large part of it came out the other side.
He flipped him over dead at his feet, beside the column.
"Monjoie!" he cried, "Barons, come forward!
Since we are doomed to die,   840
Let us defend ourselves bravely as long as we can last!"
Hearing this, Aragon thought he would go out of his mind.
He shouted, "Barons, seize them!
By Mohammed, they will soon be maimed
And tossed and thrown into the Rhône,   845
Or burned in a fire, their ashes scattered in the wind!"
Guielin said, "Barons, step aside!
For, by the apostle they seek in Nero's Meadow,
Before you take me, you will pay dearly!"
Furiously he shook his pole;   850
Count William attacked with his log
And Gilbert with his iron-tipped staff.
The brave-hearted barons struck fearsome blows:
They killed fourteen Turks
And so terrified the others   855
That they pushed them back through the gates;
They had the locks fastened and closed,
And they lifted the drawbridge with large chains.
May God, who hung on the cross, look after them!
William was now in dangerous surroundings,   860
Along with Gilbert and the valiant Guielin.

They were all enclosed in Gloriette,
And the Saracens, those mad scoundrels,
Attacked them violently and without delay.

27.
The Saracens were proud and haughty,   865
Attacking violently by the hundreds and thousands.
They let fly their lances and sharp-pointed steel javelins.
The Christians defended themselves like noble knights,
Tossing the scoundrels into ditches and trenches;
More than fourteen of them tumbled down;   870
Even the healthiest one had his neck smashed.
Seeing this, Aragon nearly lost his mind;
He nearly went mad with sorrow and anger.
With his booming voice he began to shout:
"Are you up there, proud-faced William?"   875
And the count replied, "Truly, I am here;
I took up lodging here thanks to my prowess;
May God, who was nailed to the cross, come to my aid!"

28.
Now William was inside Gloriette;
He began speaking to the Saracens: 880
"Cursed be anyone who tries to hide because of you!
I came into this city to spy;
Now I have led you along and deceived you so much
That I have driven you out of Gloriette.
From now on you will be the shepherds of this tower;   885
Guard it well and you will earn decent wages."
Hearing this, Aragon thought he would lose his mind.
He called out to the Saracens and pagans:
"To arms, quickly now, noble knights!
Let the attack begin with force!   890
Whoever can capture William the warrior
Will be the standard-bearer of my kingdom;
My entire fortune will be at his disposal!"
When his men heard this, they were joyful and glad;
The vile traitors rushed to take up their arms;   895

They attacked William in front and from behind.
Seeing this, the count thought he would lose his mind;
He called upon God, the true source of justice.

29.
Now William was irate and sorrowful,
As were Guielin and the noble Gilbert   900
In Gloriette, where they were confined.
The pagan army attacked them hard,
Hurling their lances and piercing steel arrows.
Seeing this, William nearly lost his mind.
"Guielin, my nephew, what are we waiting for?   905
We shall never return to France;
If God does not attend to this by his command,
We shall never see our cousins or relatives."
The handsome Guielin replied:
"Uncle William, you are speaking nonsense.   910
You came here for love!
Look at Orable, Tibaut of Africant's wife:
There is not a more beautiful woman alive in this world!
Go sit beside her on that bench;
Fold her in your arms   915
And don't be slow to kiss her;
For, by the apostle the penitents seek,
We shall never gain our money's worth from any kiss
Without it costing us twenty thousand silver marks,
And great suffering for our families."   920
—"God," said William, "you have so mocked me
That I am about to lose my senses!"

30.
Now William was angry and irate,
As were Gilbert and the valiant Guielin,
In Gloriette, where they were confined.   925
The despicable Saracens attacked them hard;
They defended themselves as courageous knights,
Hurling their poles and great solid clubs.
The queen called out to them, saying:

"Valiant knights, Frenchmen, do surrender!   930
The treacherous pagans are full of hatred toward you;
Soon you will see them climb the steps,
And you will all be dead, slain and dismembered!"
Hearing this, William thought he was losing his mind;
He ran to the chamber, beneath the thick branches of the pine
    tree,   935
And began lamenting to the queen:
"My lady," he said, "give me some armor,
For the love of God, who hung on the cross!
For, by St. Peter, if I live a long life,
You will be repaid most handsomely."   940
Hearing this, the lady wept with pity;
She ran immediately to her chamber
To a chest, which she opened;
She pulled out a fine saffron-colored hauberk
And a green-gold helm studded with gems.   945
She hastened to bring it all to William,
And he accepted the armor he had so desired.
He put on the hauberk and laced the helm,
And Lady Orable girded at his side the sword
That belonged to her husband, Tibaut the Slav.   950
She had never wished to give it to anyone,
Not even Aragon, who greatly desired it:
He was Tibaut's son, born of a legitimate wife.
She hung at William's neck a sturdy shield with a painted border,
Decorated with a lion wearing a gold crown;   955
She placed in his hand a strong, stout lance,
With a gonfalon attached by five golden nails.
"God," said William, "now I am well armed!
For God's sake, I beg you to take care of the others."

31.
When Guielin saw his uncle armed,   960
He ran into the lady-in-waiting's room,
Summoned her, and spoke kindly to her:
"My lady," he said, "by St. Peter of Rome,
Give me arms, because the need is great."

—"Young man," she said, "you are just a youth;   965
If you live, you will be a most worthy man.
The Avars and Hungarians hate you to death."
She came into the room and took a byrnie,
Forged by Isaac of Barcelona:
No sword could ever pierce a link of it;   970
She fitted it on his back, and Guielin's uncle was overjoyed.
She laced on the helmet of Aufar of Babylon,
The first ever king of the city of Orange;
No sword could ever smash it at all,
Nor knock off a gemstone or floral design from the carbuncle.   975
She girded him with Tornemont of Valsone's sword,
Stolen from him by the thief of Valdonne,
Who sold it to Tibaut at Voirecombe, who gave him
A thousand bezants and a thousand ounces of gold for it,
Thinking thereby to win the crown for his son.   980
She girded it upon his thigh with its long straps.
Over his shoulders she placed a round shield;
She gave him Maudoine of Valronne's spear,
With its thick shaft and long blade.
He was well armed, and Gilbert soon would be too.   985
Gloriette will be challenged this day!

32.
William and his nephew were well armed,
And Gilbert, for which they were glad and happy.
On his back they placed a strong double hauberk;
On his head they laced a helmet banded with green and gold;   990
Then they girded on a steel sword;
Over his shoulders they hung a quartered shield.
Before he had his good sharp spear,
The evil pagans had managed to fight
Their way up the stairwell on foot.   995
Count William came to strike Haucebier;
And Gilbert, the gatekeeper Maretant;
And Guielin in turn struck Turfier;
These three did not escape death.
They shattered the shafts of their enameled spears   1000

And the splinters flew up in the air;
They had to shift to their swords.
These men will soon be tried and proven!
Count William drew his steel sword;
He struck a pagan through from the rear,   1005
Slicing him in two like an olive branch;
His two halves fell to the floor of the palace.
Gilbert in turn struck Gaifier,
Sending his head onto the palace floor.
Guielin was not troubled: 1010
He gripped his sword and grasped his shield;
Anyone he attacked was condemned to death.
The pagans saw this and drew back;
The vile traitors turned to flee,
Pursued by the French, those noble warriors.   1015
They slew more than fourteen,
And all the others were so frightened
That they were pushed out the gates.
The French rushed to close and lock them,
Raised the drawbridge by its heavy chains,   1020
Which was attached and fastened to the tower.
May God, who judges all, watch over them!
Aragon saw this and thought he would lose his mind.

33.
Now William was sad and angry,
Along with Gilbert and brave Guielin;   1025
These pagan peoples were sorely harassing them:
They let fly their lances and javelins at the tower
And tore down the walls with their iron mauls.
William saw this and nearly collapsed with anger.
"Nephew Guielin," he said, "what shall we do?   1030
We will never return to France, I think,
Nor kiss our relatives and nephews."
—"Uncle William, you are wasting your breath,
Because, by the apostle they seek in Nero's Meadow,
I intend to sell myself dear before we descend!"   1035
They went down the tower stairs,

Striking those pagans on their round helmets;
They sliced through their chins and chests
And some seventeen lay dead on the sand;
The least harmed had his lung severed.   1040
The pagans saw this and their hearts trembled;
They shouted to mighty King Aragon:
"Ask for a truce, we'll never get in there!"
Aragon heard this and nearly collapsed with anger;
He swore by Mohammed that they would pay for this!   1045

34.
Aragon saw the pagans hesitate;
He called loudly and spoke to them:
"Sons of bitches, scoundrels, ill-fated was the hour you went in!
You will never hold fiefs or borderlands from me:
Fight harder if you wish to earn them!"   1050
And that they did, the infidel scoundrels:
They threw their javelins and miserable lances,
And with iron mauls destroyed all the walls.
William saw this and nearly went mad with anger.
"Nephew Guielin, whatever can we do?   1055
We are all defeated and as good as dead."
—"Uncle William, you are speaking madness,
Because, by the apostle they seek at his reliquary,
I will sell myself dear before the pagans capture me!"
The points of their spears were shattered;   1060
Each of the three of them seized an axe
That noble Lady Orable gave them.
Dressed in full armor, they went forward,
Striking those pagans on their red shields.
They sliced through their chests and faces;   1065
More than fourteen lay dead
On the marble floor, and the others fainted.
No three men had ever wreaked such havoc!
Aragon saw this and nearly went mad with anger.

35.
When Aragon saw his men suffering,   1070

He was so grief-stricken he nearly collapsed with anger.
In a clear voice he shouted loudly:
"Are you up there, noble-bodied William,
Son of Aymeri of mighty Narbonne?
Do one thing that I can think to ask: 1075
Leave Gloriette, the palace, aside,
And go away safe and sound, alive,
Before you lose your limbs and your blood.
If you don't, it will be a bad bargain for you:
By Mohammed, in whom I believe,   1080
We will make such a huge pyre of this place
That you will all be burned and grilled within!"
But William replied, "You are speaking nonsense!
We have enough bread, wine, and grain,
And cured meat and claret and spiced wine,   1085
And white hauberks and shining green-gold helms,
Good swords with silver pommels,
Sharp spears and good, weighty shields,
And beautiful women for our pleasure.
I'll not leave as long as I live;   1090
Rather, the king, noble Louis, will hear about this,
And Bernard my brother, white-haired and hoary,
And the fighter Garin from Anseaume,
Powerful Duke Beuve of Commarchis,
My nephew Bertrand, who is brave and worthy,   1095
Whom we left in Nîmes.
Each one of these, if he desires,
Can call up twenty thousand fighting men.
When they learn the truth—
That we are under siege in here—   1100
They will come nobly to our rescue
With as many men as they can gather.
Truly these walls will be no protection for you,
Nor this palace resplendent of shining gold;
You will see it shattered in a thousand pieces.   1105
If they capture you, it will be a bad bargain for you:
You will be hanged and swinging in the wind."
Said Aragon, "We will feel an immense sadness!"

Said Pharaoh, king of Bonivent:
"Emir, sire, you are not worth a glove!   1110
By Mohammed, you have little understanding:
Your father was most worthy and most brave,
Who left you guarding this city
And Gloriette, the palace, as well;
These three scoundrels are challenging you for it,   1115
And have killed your men and your people.
By Mohammed, you are worth nothing at all
If you don't burn them with stinking Greek fire!"[6]

36.
"Pharaoh, sire," said King Aragon,
"Please give me good advice, by Mohammed.   1120
Look there at Gloriette, the palace and tower:
It is built of stones all the way to the top;
All the men from here to Moncontour
Couldn't make a crack from bottom to top.
Where, by the living devil, could you start the fire?   1125
There's not a peg or stave of wood.
Those three scoundrels got in there by their audacity,
And we'll not get them out in seven years."

37.
"Pharaoh, sire," said King Aragon,
"By Mohammed, the source of our religion,   1130
Give me some good advice right now!
Look there at Gloriette, the main palace:
Its foundations are made of stone;
All the men from here to the pass of Vauquois
Couldn't crack them in a month.   1135
How the devil can you start a fire
When there isn't a peg of wood or laurel?

---

6   Greek fire was a flammable mixture made of materials such as pitch, naphtha, pine resin, and
sulfur. Because it could not be extinguished with water, Greek fire was used with great effectiveness
by the Byzantine Greeks in naval battles, and later by Muslim forces against the Crusaders.

Those three scoundrels got in there by their audacity,
And I'll not get them out in seven years!"
At that, a pagan named Orquanois came forward;   1140
His beard was black, his hair was scant,
His eyelids white, and he settled the argument.
In a clear voice he shouted three times:
"Emir, sire, listen to me!
Tell me now if I'll be rewarded   1145
If I turn over William the Frenchman to you
So you can hold him in your prison?"
Aragon replied, "Yes, by my faith.
I'll grant you ten mules laden with
Pure Spanish gold; but tell me the truth."   1150
Orquanois said, "Listen to me:
If you grant me what you've promised now,
I'll come up with a plan, no matter what."
—"I grant it to you just as you ask," Aragon answered,
"And I swear loyally at this moment   1155
That I'll give you the wealth whenever you please."
Said the pagan, "I give you my word."

38.
Orquanois said, "By Mohammed, fair sire,
Now I'll tell you how you can sneak in:
See Gloriette, this marble tower?   1160
Its foundation was laid long ago
By Griffon of Almeria,
An exceptionally clever Saracen.
You don't know what ingenious trick they used:
Below the ground is a secret passage   1165
With a sliding door into your palace.
Take a thousand Turks and go with them yourself;
Besiege the tower from the front
And invade it mightily from the back.
William will suffer and die."   1170
—"By Mohammed," Aragon said, "you tell the truth:
You shall be well rewarded, by Apollo my lord!"

39.
When Aragon heard the news
That there was a tunnel below the ground,
He was so happy that his heart leapt.   1175
He took a thousand Turks, who laced on their helmets,
And left a thousand in the square in front,
Who besieged Guielin and William.
The others set off and did not stop or rest
Until they reached the crypt;   1180
They brought candles and lanterns with them;
The filthy enemy troops entered.
The good knights did not realize a thing
Until they were well inside the palace;
William was the first to see them.   1185
"My God," said the count, "beautiful king of heaven,
We are all going to suffer and die!"
Said Guielin, "By the body of St. Hilary,
So help me God, Orable has betrayed us;
And may God confound the Saracens!"   1190

40.
Count William saw the palace fill up
With Saracens, who advanced angrily;
He saw their hauberks and helmets shining.
"By God, who is ever truthful," said the count,
"How we are condemned to suffering and death!"   1195
—"I swear, fair sir," replied Guielin,
"That bright-faced Orable has betrayed us;
May God confound the pagans and Saracens!
Today is the day our lives must end;
Let us do all we can as long as we are able: 1200
We have neither friends nor relatives here."
Count William grasped his steel sword;
Angrily he went to strike a pagan
Crosswise and cut him in half.
This blow astounded the pagans,   1205
Who attacked him angrily and furiously.
They defended themselves like bold knights;

The paladin counts gave mighty blows.
The assault was fierce, and fierce the battle,
And would not end until they were defeated.   1210
No fight was ever better fought:
Defending themselves, they killed thirty Turks.
But what does it matter, for they will not have the last word!
Pagans and Saracens took them in hand,
Turks, Persians, and Almoravids,   1215
As well as Acoparts, Esclamors, and Bedouins.
They swore by Mohammed that vengeance would be taken:
Today they will avenge the deaths of their friends.

41.
William was captured by mortal treason,
Along with Gilbert and brave Guielin.   1220
The wicked Saracens had them in their grasp;
They swore by Mohammed to take vengeance on them.
They sent to the city for twenty young men
And had a large, deep ditch dug.
In it they laid kindling and logs,   1225
Because they wanted to grill our barons.
Fair-faced Orable came forward
And spoke to her son-in-law Aragon:
"Friend," she said, "turn these prisoners over to me,
And I will put them in the depths of my jail.   1230
There are toads and snakes that will eat them all,
And serpents that will devour them."
—"My lady queen," said King Aragon,
"You brought all this trouble upon us
When you armed these scoundrels up there.   1235
May anyone who turns them over to you be cursed by
    Mohammed!"
The lady heard this and nearly collapsed with anger.
"Son of a bitch, scoundrel, you'll be sorry!
By Mohammed whom I pray to and adore,
Were it not for these other barons   1240
I'd slug you in the nose with my fist!
Get out of my tower at once;

Woe is you if you stay any longer!"
She addressed the wicked traitor:
"Rascal," she said, "put them in your prison   1245
Until Tibaut returns from Valdon,
Along with Desramé and Goliath the blond.
They will take what vengeance they please."
—"So it shall be, my lady," said King Aragon.
They threw William into the deep cell,   1250
Along with Guielin and Gilbert the brave.
Let us turn now from these barons;
When the time is right, we shall get back to them;
Now we shall sing of the pagan hordes.

42.
King Aragon was not reassured.   1255
He gathered his messengers and sent them across the seas.
They set off and did not rest or slow down,
And did not stop until they reached the Rhône.
There they entered their ship,
A boat belonging to Maudoine of Nubia.   1260
It was masterfully covered with silk
And did not fear storm or tempest.
They raised anchor, hoisted their sails,
Sailed away from the town and put out to sea.
They glided, rowed, navigated, and cruised;   1265
They had a good wind to blow them straight on.
They reached the port below Almeria,
Where they cast anchor and lowered their sails.
They mounted horses and rode without stopping,
Without resting or slowing down,   1270
Until they entered the city of Africant.
They dismounted in the shade of an olive tree
And ascended to the stone hall,
Where they found Tibaut and his pagan people;
They greeted him in the Saracen manner: 1275
"May Mohammed, who rules over all,
Save King Tibaut of Esclavonia!
Your proud-faced son summons you

To rescue him with your knights.
He has captured William, I'll not hide it from you,   1280
The son of mighty Aymeri of Narbonne,
In Orange, that opulent city.
William entered the town in disguise,
Thinking to capture it as he had Nîmes,
And to win Lady Orable as his lover.   1285
But they couldn't pull off this devilish scheme.
He nearly defeated us within Gloriette,
Holding her there for seven days.
Had it not been for the underground passage,
Made of stone beneath the palace,   1290
You would never again have Orable,
Your most gracious wife.
But Mohammed came to your rescue,
For we have William isolated in a cell
From which he will never escape.   1295
Whatever vengeance you please will be taken."
Hearing this, Tibaut began to laugh;
He summoned the people of his empire:
"To arms quickly, brave and noble knights!"
They took them up without delay   1300
And mounted their Russian and Apulian horses.
When Tibaut left the city of Africant,
He took with him the pagans of Almeria,
And those of Susce and Esclavonia.
There were sixty thousand in the vanguard;   1305
They did not slow down or stop until they reached the sea.
In short order the ships were supplied
With wine, meat, biscuit, and grain.
This Saracen army embarked,
Raised their anchors, and hoisted their sails.   1310
The wind filled them and blew their ships straight on;
They put out to sea and sailed their route.
At that time you could hear so many horns and trumpets,
Bears growling and hounds yapping,
Mules braying and horses neighing,   1315
Sparrowhawks singing on their perches:

They could all be heard from a good league away.
They sailed for eight days, even nine,
But before they reached powerful Orange
Tibaut will feel more grief and anger   1320
Than he ever felt in all the days of his life,
For he will lose his strong fortified city
And his wife, slender Orable.

43.
William was deep in the jail,
Along with Gilbert and noble Guielin.   1325
"God," said the count, "dear Father, loving king,
How we are condemned to death and suffering!
God! If only the king, noble Louis, knew about this,
And Bernard my brother, white-haired and hoary,
And the fighter Garin from Anseaume,   1330
Powerful Duke Beuve of Commarchis,
My nephew Bertrand, who is brave and worthy,
Whom we left outside Nîmes
With twenty thousand fighting Frenchmen.
We are in great need of their help!"   1335
Guielin, the handsome and noble, said,
"Uncle William, you are speaking nonsense.
Send word to Orable, the wife of the Africant,
To use her love to help her lover."
—"By God," said William, "you have mocked me so   1340
That my heart is near to breaking."

44.
Now William was angry and downcast,
Along with Gilbert and brave Guielin,
Down in the cell making a loud racket.
While they were lamenting in this way,   1345
Orable came down to enter the cell;
When she saw the counts, she addressed them:
"Listen to me, fair and noble knights.
The pagans and Saracens bear you a mortal hatred:
They will hang you tonight or in the morning."   1350

—"We can do nothing, my lady," said Guielin.
"Please find some way, fair and noble lady,
To release us from this prison!
I would become your sworn and dutiful man,
And will serve you most willingly   1355
Whenever you please. Noble lady, take pity!"
—"Truly," said William, "she betrayed us,
And it is by her doing that we have been locked in this cell."
The lady heard this and sighed.

45.
"Lordly barons," said courtly Orable,   1360
"By Mohammed, you are wrong to blame me:
I gave you arms in this tower.
If you could keep up the fight in this palace
Long enough for Charles's son Louis to hear of it,
And Sir Bernard of Brabant and the others,   1365
And Aymeri and your mighty lineage,
The infidel scoundrels wouldn't learn of it
Until your people were within this fine tower.
In that way they could win this borderland
And these narrows, fords, and passes."   1370
—"My lady, you speak well," said Guielin.
"If we were freed from this cell,
I would be your servant the rest of my life."
—"By my faith," said Queen Orable,
"If I thought that my efforts would be rewarded—   1375
That William Fierebrace would take me—
I would release all three of you from this cell
And would immediately become Christian!"
William heard this and his heart lit up within him.
"My lady," he said, "I give you my pledge: 1380
I promise you this by God and St. James,
And by the apostle they seek at his reliquary."
—"In truth," said the lady, "I ask no other pledge."
She unlocked all the doors to the cell
And they, who were so very valiant, came out;   1385
Each was overjoyed in his heart.

46.

Now the lady has offered the counts her protection;
She has released all three from the cell
And has guided and taken them into Gloriette.
Up in the palace they sat down to dinner;   1390
Once they were lavishly served,
The noble lady spoke to them:
"Lordly barons, listen to me:
Now I have released you from my prison
And have guided and brought you up to the palace;   1395
Now I don't know how to escape from here.
But I must tell you what I think:
Under us there is a passageway
That no one knows about,
Except my ancestors who had it dug;   1400
It runs from here to the Rhône.
If you were to send a messenger now
To Count Bertrand and the other barons,
They could come underground to speak with you
And the infidel pagans wouldn't know about it   1405
Until they were up in the stone palace,
Where they could strike with the swords at their sides,
And that way could win the city
And the narrows, gates, and fords."
And William said, "My lady, that is true!   1410
But I don't know where to find a messenger."

47.

"Nephew Guielin," said Count William,
"Don't slow down or stop until you reach Nîmes;
You will tell your brother Bertrand
To rescue me with the men of his land."   1415
—"Uncle William," said Guielin, "enough!
So help me God, you must be joking,
Because, by the faith I owe St. Stephen,
I would rather die in this beautiful tower
Than in sweet France or Aix-la-Chapelle."   1420

48.

"Nephew Guielin," said noble William,
"You will enter the secret passageway
And not stop until you reach Nîmes.
You will tell the paladin Bertrand on my behalf
To come to my rescue immediately!"   1425
—"Uncle William, you are speaking nonsense;
I wouldn't leave you if I lost my limbs!
I would rather die within this tower
Than in sweet France or with my relatives.
Send Gilbert the Fleming."   1430
—"Will you go there, brother?" asked noble William.
And the baron replied, "I will go in truth
And deliver your message faithfully."
—"Go then, fair brother; I commend you to Jesus.
You will tell the paladin Bertrand   1435
To rescue me; don't delay!
And if you don't, by the loving God,
His nephew will never again see William!"

49.

When the messenger heard that he must go,
He began to complain loudly   1440
That he could not escape the tower
"For I have never been there and don't know where to go."
And the lady replied, "I believe I can guide you well;
You need not fear any man alive,
Except for Jesus in majesty."   1445
She had a large stone removed from beside a pillar;
It was a good six feet in length and width.
"Brother," she said, "you can enter through here.
At the end you will find three pillars,
Made and carved with vaulted arches."   1450
Gilbert set off and began to wander
Beneath the city, he knew not where.
Count William, Lady Orable,
And Guielin accompanied the baron;

They did not stop until they reached the three pillars.   1455
He crossed through the midst of them
And came to the Rhône, where he found a boat;
He swiftly rowed himself across.
Count William, Guielin,
And fair-faced Orable turned back;   1460
All three went back into Gloriette.
They would have been better off
To have gone back down into the cell,
Because everything they had discussed and done
Had been overheard by a Saracen.   1465
He went to report it to King Aragon.

50.
The Saracen was extremely sly;
He went to announce it all to King Aragon.
As soon as he saw him, he spoke to him:
"Emir, sire, be silent and hear   1470
How your stepmother behaved
Toward the captives you had in your prison:
She has released all three from the cell
And has guided and taken them into the palace;
Up in Gloriette they sat down to dinner."   1475
Aragon asked, "Are you telling the truth, messenger?"
—"My lord," he replied, "I am not a liar.
I saw them huddling together in conversation,
And her hugging and kissing each one in turn.
She loves them all, especially William in her bed,   1480
More than your father or King Haucebier."
Aragon heard this and thought he would lose his mind.
He summoned Saracens and Slavs:
"Barons," he said, "advise me
How I should behave   1485
Toward my stepmother who has humiliated me so,
Shaming me and disgracing my father."

51.
Aragon said, "Noble and courageous knights,

By Mohammed, take up your arms at once!
Know that those receiving arms here   1490
Will capture the Christians at great cost."
They replied, "As you order!"
Fifteen thousand men ran to put on their armor.
God! what a pity that William
And Lady Orable and valiant Guielin did not know this.   1495
In Gloriette where they were hidden
They were playing chess, all reassured;
The brave-hearted counts were caught unaware
When the Saracens and Slavs attacked them.

52.
Aragon found William beneath the pine tree,   1500
Along with Lady Orable and brave Guielin.
The paladin knights had no idea
That the pagans and Saracens,
Turks, Persians, and wicked Bedouins were upon them.
These swore by Mohammed that they would have vengeance;   1505
Pharaoh, who considered himself the sharpest,
Said, "Emir, sire, listen to me:
Your father Tibaut, who left you
This city and Gloriette the stately palace
To hold, is brave and noble.   1510
These scoundrels have challenged you,
Killed your men, slaughtering and slaying them.
By Mohammed, you aren't worth a cent
If you don't have them torn limb from limb;
And if you don't have your stepmother,   1515
Who's shamed us, burned and grilled over a fire!"
Said elderly white-haired Esquanor:
"King Pharaoh, you have not spoken well."

53.
Said white-haired elderly Esquanor:
"King Pharaoh, you have not judged well.   1520
You should not promote foolishness:
If you start it, it's hard to stop.

Emir, sire, be quiet and listen to me.
Your father Tibaut, who left you
This city and Gloriette, the palace and fief,   1525
To guard, is a perfect knight.
If you were to burn his wife,
He would be angry with you at once.
Instead, have these counts thrown into your prison
And Lady Orable tossed in as well.   1530
Take your messenger and send him across the sea.
Your father and King Haucebier will come
And immediately take their vengeance."
Said Aragon, "You have judged well;
You will be richly rewarded and lack for nothing.   1535
But I have already sent the messenger
To my father the king who rules Africa;
He will be back here in less than a week."
They had William thrown into the cell,
And brave and agile Guielin;   1540
And Lady Orable was tossed in with them.
May God who judges all watch over them!

54.
Now William was thrown into the cell
Along with Guielin and courtly Orable;
She often regretted her unhappy state: 1545
"God," said the lady, "dear Father in heaven,
Why has this poor woman not yet been baptized?
I hoped to be, and to believe in God.
Sir William, woe to me when I saw your nobility,
Your fair body, and your courage,   1550
And am thrown into this cell because of you,
In such anguish as if I'd been defiled."
Said Guielin, "You are speaking folly.
You and my uncle are at great ease now,
Your great love should see you through this trouble!"   1555
William heard this and nearly went mad with grief;
In his anger he swore by St. James:
"If it weren't a vile and shameful thing,

I'd give you a mighty blow!"
—"That would be foolish," said Guielin,   1560
"Today I'll say, and I don't care who knows:
They used to call you William Fierebrace,
But now they'll say William the Lover!
It was love that brought you into this city."
The count heard him and lowered his head.   1565

55.
Now William was sad and angry,
Along with Lady Orable and Guielin his nephew,
In the cell into which they had been thrown.
"God," said the count, "glorious king of heaven,
How we've been tricked, betrayed, and left for dead!   1570
By what folly was this affair started,
Which has brought us shame and disgrace,
Unless he who judges all looks down upon us?
Alas, if only proud King Louis knew of this,
And my elderly white-haired brother Bernard,   1575
And the esteemed Sir Garin of Anseaume,
And Bertrand the strong in Nîmes;
We could have great use of their help!"
—"Uncle William," said proud Guielin,
"Let it be, for it's no use now.   1580
Look at Orable, the courtly woman,
You can hug and kiss her easily;
One couldn't ask for a more beautiful woman."
—"God," said the count, "I'm about to go mad!"
The pagans heard them arguing in the cell;   1585
More than forty hurried there,
Who released the two of them from the cell.
They left Orable, the courtly woman,
And took the uncle and nephew to the palace;
Pharaoh, at his haughtiest, spoke to Aragon: 1590
"Emir, sire, be quiet and listen to me:
Your father Tibaut, who left you
This city and Gloriette, the palace and the fief,
To hold, is most worthy of praise.

Look at this scoundrel, this young man: 1595
He doesn't give a penny for anything you say.
By Mohammed, you're no better than a shepherd
If you don't have him torn limb from limb,
Him and his uncle William, the fighter!"
Guielin heard him and thought he would lose his mind.   1600
He ground his teeth and rolled his eyes;
After rolling up his sleeves, he stepped forward
And grabbed Pharaoh by the hair with his left fist;
He raised his right fist and hit him on the neck,
Breaking his jaw in two   1605
And knocking him dead at his feet.
William saw this and was overjoyed.
"God," said the count, "you who are judge over all,
How we are fated to suffer and die!"

56.
William saw Pharaoh fall.   1610
"God," said the count, "dear king of paradise,
How we are condemned to suffering and death!"
—"Don't be upset, uncle," said Guielin,
"You are not without friends in this palace."
—"In truth," said William, "there are few!"   1615
Then young Guielin looked about
And saw a large axe beside a pillar;
He stepped forward, seized it with both hands,
And went to strike a barbarous pagan,
Splitting him all the way to his chest.   1620
Aragon saw this and thought he would go mad;
He cried out, "Seize them, Saracens!
By Mohammed, they will suffer
And be thrown and tossed into the Rhône!"
Said Guielin, "Scoundrel, get out of here!   1625
You have released us from the cell
And have led and brought us to the palace.
But, by the apostle who is sainted in Rome,
You have gathered companions here
Who will cause you grief and suffering."   1630

At these words there appeared two Saracens
Carrying a large container of wine by a pole;
They planned to serve it up in the palace,
But when they saw the powerful blows being struck,
They turned to flee and let the wine fall.   1635
Count William rushed to seize the pole,
Taking it at once in his two hands;
With it he gave mighty blows to pagans and Saracens;
Everyone he struck fell to the ground.

57.
Now William was in the stone-floored palace,   1640
Along with his nephew Guielin the illustrious.
One held the axe, the other the pole;
The brave-hearted warriors landed mighty blows.
They killed fourteen Turks
And so frightened all the others   1645
That they drove them out through the gates.
Then they rushed to secure and lock them
And raised the drawbridge with heavy chains.
Aragon saw this and thought he would lose his mind.
He summoned Saracens and Slavs: 1650
"Advise me, for the sake of Mohammed my god!
This William has treated me badly
In taking my princely palace from me.
Now I can see no way to enter it!"
Let us turn now from the Saracens;   1655
We must sing next of Gilbert,
The messenger who has crossed the Rhône.
He climbs the hills and crosses the valleys
And does not stop until he reaches Nîmes.
Count Bertrand had risen early   1660
And climbed to the palace of the infidel Otrant
That he had won by his imposing courage.
He was leaning upon the broad windowsills
And looked out across the kingdom;
He saw the green grass and the rose gardens,   1665
And heard the oriole and the blackbird singing.

Then he remembered short-nosed William
And his brother Guielin the illustrious.
He began to weep most tenderly
And lamented them, as you can hear now: 1670
"Uncle William, you were foolish
To go to reconnoiter Orange
Disguised as a wandering pilgrim.
Brother Guielin, how brave you were,
But now the Saracens and Slavs have slain you. 1675
I am all alone back here in this land
And see no one of my powerful lineage
From whom I can obtain good advice.
The Slavs and Goliath and King Desramé
And Clareau and his brother Aceré, 1680
And Aguisant and King Giboez
And the Saracen chief of Royaumont by the Sea,
And Kings Eubron, Bourreau, and Lorrez,
And Quinzepaumes and his brother Gondrez,
The thirty kings born in Spain, 1685
Are all about to come back here.
Each will bring thirty thousand armed soldiers
And will attack me in the citadel of Nîmes;
They will take me by sheer force,
And I will be slaughtered, killed, or slain. 1690
But on one point I have made a decision:
The gold of ten cities will not prevent me
From returning to the land of my birth
And bringing back with me my barons
Whom short-nosed William took with him. 1695
When I reach the city of Paris,
I shall dismount at the enameled block of stone;
Young men and sergeants will approach
And will ask me about William,
And about my brother the valiant Guielin. 1700
Alas, woe is me! I won't know what to say,
Except that pagans have killed them in Orange."
He fainted twice upon the marble staircase,
And the barons rushed to lift him back up.

58.
Count Bertrand was very sad, grieving   1705
For Guielin and noble William;
He lamented them handsomely and courteously:
"Uncle William, you were a fool
When you went to Orange as you did,
Disguised as a wandering pilgrim;   1710
Brother Guielin, how noble you were!
But now the Saracens and Persians have slain you.
I am all alone here in this pagan land:
I have no cousin or relative with me.
Soon King Tibaut of Africant,   1715
Desramé, and the giant Goliath,
And the thirty kings will return with their reinforcements.
They will attack me here in Nîmes
And I will suffer and die.
But, by the apostle the penitents seek,   1720
I would rather lose my limbs
Than fail to go to mighty Orange
And avenge the grief and suffering
That the Saracens have caused our people.
Alas, woe is me! What am I waiting for   1725
That I don't set off at once to help them?"

59.
Count Bertrand was sad and filled with anger.
While he was weeping and sighing,
Behold, Gilbert entered the town
And climbed the staircase of the marble hall.   1730
Bertrand saw him and began to laugh;
In his clear voice he shouted to him:
"You are most welcome, brave and noble knight!
Where is my proud-faced uncle?
And Guielin? Don't hide it from me."   1735
Gilbert replied like a noble knight:
"In Orange, that splendid city,
In Gloriette, the marble tower;
Wicked pagans are holding and persecuting them,

And any minute I expect them both to be killed.   1740
I'll not hide anything: William asks
That you come quickly with your knights
To rescue him without any delay!"
Bertrand heard him and began to laugh;
So that all could hear, he summoned his empire: 1745
"To arms, quickly, brave and noble knights!"
And they took up their arms without delay;
They mounted their Spanish and Syrian horses.
When Bertrand left the city of Nîmes,
He led with him the men of his empire;   1750
In the vanguard were more than fifteen thousand,
And they did not stop until they reached the Rhône.
Everyone embarked on the ships and galleys;
The French rowed, navigated, and sailed.
The brave companies landed   1755
Below Orange, in the vast prairie;
They set up tents and erected pavilions.
Count Bertrand did not delay a moment;
As soon as he saw the messenger, he said to him:
"Sir Gilbert, don't lie to me,   1760
Shall we attack this city of Orange?
Can we destroy these walls and marble halls?"
Gilbert replied, "You are speaking nonsense,
Because it can resist the entire French empire;
You won't capture it in your lifetime!"   1765
Bertrand heard this and nearly went mad with anger.

60.
"Gilbert, brother," said Count Bertrand,
"Shall we attack Orange the indomitable?
Can we destroy these walls and mighty fortifications?"
Gilbert replied, "You are speaking nonsense;   1770
You will not capture it as long as you live."
Bertrand became upset with this answer,
Until the messenger comforted him:
"My lord," he said, "listen to my thought:
I shall sneak you into the city in such a way   1775

That the Saracens and Persians will not know it."
—"Go ahead, dear brother; I commend you to Jesus."
Knowing the situation, he set off
With thirteen thousand Frenchmen,
Leaving the others in their tents and shelters.   1780
They did not stop until they reached the tunnel;
They entered between the pillars;
With no candles or flaming torches
They went single file through the deep darkness.
Bertrand was extremely worried;   1785
He summoned the messenger and said aloud:
"Gilbert, brother, don't keep anything from me:
I believe that my uncle is dead
And you've sold us to the infidels."
Gilbert replied, "You are speaking nonsense;   1790
I'd lose my limbs before betraying you.
You will soon be up in Gloriette;
For God's sake, please keep quiet!"
—"Lead on, dear brother, by God's command."
While they were yet speaking in this manner   1795
They came to Gloriette;
Count William saw them first.
"My God," said the count, "dear Father, heavenly king,
Now I see the solution I was so longing for!"
The brave knights removed their helmets,   1800
Kissed one another, and wept with joy.
Count Bertrand spoke to William:
"How is it, uncle? Don't keep it from me."
—"Very well, fair nephew, thanks to almighty God.
I have suffered great pain and deprivation;   1805
I never thought I'd see you again in my lifetime.
The Saracens and Persians have tortured me so!"
—"Uncle William, you will soon be avenged!"
Up in the palace they sounded a trumpet;
Below, they were arming themselves in the tents and shelters.   1810
Count William was brave and courageous.
They lowered the drawbridges at once,
Came to the gates of the splendid city,

Opened them quickly and easily;
Those outside swarmed through them, 1815
Crying "Monjoie" on every side.
The pagans were frightened by this joy;
The filthy traitors ran to arm themselves
And rushed out of their dwellings,
Hastily armed in order to defend themselves. 1820
But their effort was worthless,
For there were too many Frenchmen:
Bertrand had recaptured the whole city.
There you could have witnessed a mighty battle
To regain the strong, noble city: 1825
So many shafts shattered, so many shields crushed,
So many Algerian hauberks torn apart,
So many Saracens dead in a bloody heap!
When Aragon saw his people slain,
He was so grief-stricken he nearly lost his senses. 1830
He leapt into the saddle of his powerful warhorse,
Took a shield he had captured from a Frenchman,
Looked down and saw a sharp spear on the ground,
Leaned down and took it by both hands;
He urged his horse on with his sharp spurs 1835
And struck in the middle of the great battle.
There he killed our Foucher of Meliant,
Then a second and a third Frenchman.
Bertrand saw this and nearly lost his senses.
He drew his sword with its sharp cutting edge, 1840
Struck Aragon, showing no mercy;
In his anger he gave him such a mighty blow
That he split him open down to his chest;
He knocked him dead from his powerful warhorse.
The pagans lost their strength and courage. 1845
Why should I make my story any longer?
No pagan escaped death
A river of blood ran along the ground.
Count William did not hesitate:
He came immediately to the prison cell 1850

And released Orable, the lady with the worthy body.
He summoned Bertrand and said to him, so all could hear:
"Fair nephew," he said, "listen to my thoughts
About this beautiful and comely lady
Who truly saved my life: 1855
I pledged my word to her in all honesty
That I would truly take her as my wife."
Bertrand replied, "What are you waiting for?
Fulfill all your promise to her
And marry her with great joy!"   1860
—"Nephew," said William, "as you command!"

61.
Count William was very noble and valiant.
After he had won the city in battle,
He had a large vat made ready,
Filled with fresh water.   1865
The bishop of the city of Nîmes was there.
They had Orable strip off her clothing
And baptized her to the honor of God.
They removed her pagan name;
Bertrand and valiant Guielin and Gilbert,   1870
The brave and wise, held her over the font;
They gave her the Christian name of Guibourc.
In a church they had just had dedicated,
Where Mohammed had once been worshipped,
Count William married her.   1875
Bishop Gaimar sang mass for them.
After mass they left the church
And brought the lady to Gloriette;
There was a magnificent celebration in the paved palace.
Count Bertrand served their dinner,   1880
Along with Gilbert and valiant Guielin.
The joyous festivities lasted a whole week.
There were numerous harpists and jongleurs,
Silk cloths and capes of ermine,
Spanish mules and swift horses.   1885

62.

Count William married the lady;
He resided thirty more years in Orange,
But never a day without combat.

Glossary

Adze: Hand tool generally used for squaring up construction timber.

Almoner: Religious functionary responsible for distributing alms.

Bezant: Byzantine gold coin worth about two dozen deniers or two sous.

Boss: Circular prominence in the center of a shield to deflect weapons.

Brazier: Open pan for holding hot coals and for cooking when in the field.

Breeches: Wide cloth drawers worn by men as under or outer clothing.

Breviary: Book containing the daily prayers recited or read at canonical hours (q.v.) throughout the year; cf. *missal, psalter.*

Buckler: Small round shield.

Buckram: Coarse cotton fabric.

Burgher: Citizen of a burg, or town.

Byrnie: Coat of mail, also called a hauberk (q.v.).

Canon: Member of the chapter of a cathedral or a male religious house; also, rule or law enacted by a church council.

Canonical hours: The seven official prayer hours of a medieval day—matins and lauds, prime, terce, sext, nones, vespers, and compline—set by canon law.

Carbuncle: Red garnet cut without facets, usually used to decorate helmets.

Censer: Religious vessel for burning incense.

Chamberlain: Chief steward responsible for the household affairs of a medieval noble.

Chancel: Space near the altar of a church, reserved for clergy and choir.

Claret: Dry red wine, usually from the Bordeaux region.

Cleric: Member of the clergy, men set apart by ordination for the service of God.

Coffer: Chest or box, especially one for holding valuables.

Coif: Hood of chain mail that pulled over the head, worn with a hauberk (q.v.).

Cope: Long semicircular mantle worn by nobles and clerics.

Fealty: Obligation of fidelity owed by a vassal to his feudal lord, also implying service in time of war.

Fief, fiefdom: Landed estate held by a vassal under another noble or the king.

Galangal: Aromatic rootstalk of an herb of the ginger family.

Galley: Long, low vessel propelled by oars and a sail, or by oars alone.

Goad: Pointed stick for driving oxen or other beasts.

Gonfalon: Banner or pennant, usually long and tapered, affixed to a lance or other weapon to identify a knight.

Gorget: Piece of armor to protect the throat.

Hauberk: Coat of mail composed of interlocking links, usually weighing about sixty pounds, mid-thigh length, short-sleeved, and generally worn with a coif (q.v.).

Helm: Helmet worn to protect the head, in our period conical and generally equipped with a bar to protect the nose.

Hilt: Handle of a sword, dagger, or similar weapon.

Hyssop: Medicinal and culinary herb of the mint family.

Javelin: Light spear thrown as a weapon.

Jongleur: Wandering entertainer of medieval Europe who earned his living singing or relating lyric songs, epic poems, and the like.

Laburnum: Hardwood from a small tree native to Europe.

Mace: Heavy medieval war club, usually with a spiked metal head, used against armored enemies.

Mantle: Loose, usually sleeveless garment worn over other clothing; a cloak or cope.

Maul: Heavy iron mallet; a sledgehammer.

Missal: Book containing all the prayers for celebrating mass throughout the yearly cycle; cf. *breviary, psalter.*

Paladin: Any of the Twelve Peers of Charlemagne; more generally, a worthy knight.

Palfrey: Saddle horse.

Palmer: Pilgrim; more specifically, one who visited the Holy Land and brought back a palm branch.

Peer: Any of the twelve nobles of Charlemagne's entourage; more generally, any male noble.

Phylactery: In medieval Europe, a case containing a relic.

Pommel: Knob on the hilt of a sword or dagger.

Psalter: Book containing the psalms; cf. *breviary, missal*.

Rear guard: Company of fighting men who protect the rear of a marching army; cf. *vanguard*.

Saddle girth: Strap that secures the saddle by passing under the horse's belly.

Seigneury: Territory belonging to a lord; rights attached to a fief.

Seneschal: Steward responsible for running the domestic affairs of a noble, administering justice, and representing him at court.

Sexton: Lower-level church official in charge of ringing bells, funerals, grave digging, and the like.

Squire: Aspirant to knighthood serving as an attendant to a knight.

Tumbrel: Rustic cart, usually having two wheels and pulled by an ox.

Vanguard: Company of fighting men who march at the head of an advancing army; cf. *rear guard*.

Vassal: Within the medieval feudal system, a person holding land from an overlord and owing him fealty, generally in the form of military service.

Vavasor: Vassal holding lands from a greater vassal or lord.

Ventail: Adjustable lower front of a helmet.

Vespers: Sixth of the seven canonical hours (q.v.) of a medieval day, recited or sung at nightfall.

Select Bibliography

Editions and Translations

Chansons de geste: Roland, Aimeri de Narbonne, Le Couronnement de Louis. Translated by Léon Clédat. 1989. Paris: Classiques Garnier, 2010.

Le Charroi de Nîmes: An English Translation with Notes. Translated by Henri J. Godin. Oxford: Blackwell, 1936.

Le Charroi de Nîmes: Chanson de geste du XIIe siècle. Edited by Duncan McMillan. 2nd ed. Paris: Klincksieck, 1978.

Le Charroi de Nîmes. Edited and translated by Claude Lachet. Paris: Gallimard, 1999.

Le Couronnement de Louis. Translated by André Lanly. Traductions des Classiques du moyen âge 6. 1969. Paris: Champion, 2013.

The Crowning of Louis: A New Metrical Translation of the Old French Verse Epic. Edited and translated by Nirmal Dass. Jefferson, NC: McFarland, 2003.

Le Cycle de Guillaume d'Orange: Anthologie. Translated by Dominique Boutet, with excerpts from editions by Perrier et al. Paris: Librairie Générale Française, 1996.

Guillaume d'Orange: Four Twelfth-Century Epics. Translated by Joan M. Ferrante. New York: Columbia University Press, 1974.

Heroines of the French Epic: A Second Selection of Chansons de Geste. Translated by Michael A. H. Newth. Cambridge: D. S. Brewer, 2014.

La Prise d'Orange: Chanson de geste (fin XIIe–début XIIIe siècle). Edited and translated by Claude Lachet. Paris: Champion Classiques, 2010.

Les Rédactions en vers de La Prise d'Orange. Edited by Claude Régnier. 2nd ed. Paris: Klincksieck, 1966.

Les Rédactions en vers du Couronnement de Louis. Edited by Yvan G. Lepage. Geneva: Droz, 1978.

Riggs, Elizabeth P. *La Prise d'Orange or William in Love: A Study and Translation of an Old French Epic of the William Cycle.* PhD diss., Columbia University, 1971.

The Song of Roland. Translated by Glyn Burgess. London: Penguin Classics, 1990.

William, Count of Orange: Four Old French Epics. Translated by Glanville Price. London: Dent; Totowa, NJ: Rowman and Littlefield, 1975.

Old French Language

Andrieux-Reix, Nelly. *Ancien français: Fiches de vocabulaire.* Paris: PUF, 1987.

Flori, Jean. "Qu'est-ce qu'un *bacheler?* Étude historique de vocabulaire dans les chansons de geste du XIIe siècle." *Romania* 96 (1975): 289–314.

Godefroy, Frédéric. *Dictionnaire de l'ancienne langue française et de tous ses dialectes du IXe au XVe siècle.* 10 vols. 1880–1902. Paris: Librairie des Sciences et des Arts, 1937–38.

Hindley, Alan, Frederick W. Langley, and Brian J. Levy. *Old French–English Dictionary.* Cambridge: Cambridge University Press, 2000.

Kibler, William W. *An Introduction to Old French.* New York: Modern Language Association, 1984.

Raynaud de Lage, Guy. *Manuel pratique d'ancien français.* Paris: Picard, 1973.

Reference Tools

Bennett, Philip E. *The Cycle of Guillaume d'Orange or Garin de Monglane: A Critical Bibliography.* Research Bibliographies and Checklists: New Series 6. Woodbridge, Suffolk: Tamesis, 2004.

Bulletin bibliographique de la Société Rencesvals pour l'étude des épopées romanes. Paris: Nizet, 1958–.

Moisan, André. *Répertoire des noms propres de personnes et de lieux cités dans les chansons de geste françaises et les œuvres étrangères dérivées.* 5 vols. Geneva: Droz, 1986.

Suard, François. *Guide de la chanson de geste et de sa postérité littéraire (XIe–XVe siècle).* Paris: Champion, 2011.

Literary Studies

Bennett, Philip E. *Carnaval héroïque et écriture cyclique dans la geste de Guillaume d'Orange.* Paris: Champion, 2006.

————. *La Chanson de Guillaume* and *La Prise d'Orange*. Critical Guides to French Texts. London: Grant & Cutler, 2000.

Colby-Hall, Alice. "In Search of Lost Epics of the Lower Rhône Valley." *Olifant* 8 (1981): 339–51.

Collomp, Denis. "*Le Couronnement de Louis* et les tiroirs de l'histoire." In Hüe, *Lectures du "Couronnement de Louis,"* 21–37.

Corbellari, Alain. *Guillaume d'Orange ou la naissance du héros médiéval*. Paris: Klincksieck, 2011.

Daniel, Norman. *Heroes and Saracens: An Interpretation of the Chansons de geste*. Edinburgh: Edinburgh University Press, 1984.

————. *Islam and the West: The Making of an Image*. Edinburgh: Edinburgh University Press, 1960.

de Weever, Jacqueline. *Sheba's Daughters: Whitening and Demonizing the Saracen Woman in Medieval French Epic*. New York: Garland, 1998.

Duggan, Joseph J. "Medieval Epic as Popular Historiography: Appropriation of Historical Knowledge in the Vernacular Epic." *Grundriß der romanischen Literaturen des Mittelalters* 11.1 (1986): 285–311.

Frappier, Jean. *Les Chansons de geste du cycle de Guillaume d'Orange*. Vol. 2, *Le Couronnement de Louis, Le Charroi de Nîmes, La Prise d'Orange*. Paris: Société d'édition d'enseignement supérieur, 1965.

Heinemann, Edward A. "L'art de la laisse dans le *Charroi de Nîmes*." In *"Contez me tout": Mélanges de langue et de littérature médiévales offerts à Herman Braet*, edited by Catherine Bel, Pascale Dumont, and Frank Willaert, 217–28. Louvain: Peeters, 2006.

————. *L'art métrique de la chanson de geste: Essai sur la musicalité du récit*. Geneva: Droz, 1993.

Hüe, Denis, ed. *Lectures du "Couronnement de Louis."* Rennes: Presses Universitaires de Rennes, 2013.

Jones, Catherine M. *An Introduction to the Chansons de Geste*. Gainesville: University Press of Florida, 2014.

Kay, Sarah. *The Chansons de Geste in the Age of Romance: Political Fictions*. Oxford: Clarendon Press, 1995.

Kinoshita, Sharon. *Medieval Boundaries: Rethinking Difference in Old French Literature*. Philadelphia: University of Pennsylvania Press, 2006.

Kullmann, Dorothea. "Le Prologue du *Couronnement de Louis* et le motif du vilain jongleur." In Hüe, *Lectures du "Couronnement de Louis"* 223–34.

Labande, Edmond-René. "Le credo épique: À propos des prières dans les chansons de geste." In *Recueil de travaux offert à M. Clovis Brunel*, edited by Mario Roques and Joseph Vendrys, 2: 62–80. Paris: Société de l'École des chartes, 1955.

Lachet, Claude. "Quelques échos structurants et signifiants dans *Le Couronnement de Louis.*" In Hüe, *Lectures du "Couronnement de Louis,"* 65–77.

Lefèvre, Yves. "*L'arche* de Saint-Pierre de Rome dans le *Couronnement de Louis.*" *Romania* 90 (1969): 111–21.

Legros, Huguette. "Le personnage de Guillaume dans *Le Couronnement de Louis* entre tradition et innovation." In Hüe, *Lectures du "Couronnement de Louis,"* 165–78.

Leverage, Paula. *Reception and Memory: A Cognitive Approach to the Chansons de geste.* Faux Titre 349. Amsterdam: Rodopi, 2010.

Martin, Jean-Pierre. *Les motifs dans la chanson de geste: Définition et utilisation.* Lille: Centre d'Études Médiévales et Dialectales, Université de Lille III, 1992.

Parry, Milman. "Studies in the Epic Technique of Oral Verse-Making. I. Homer and Homeric Style." *Harvard Studies in Classical Philology* 41 (1930): 73–147.

Ramey, Lynn Tarte. *Christian, Saracen and Genre in Medieval French Literature.* New York: Routledge, 2001.

Rossi, Marguerite. "La prière de demande dans l'épopée." In *La Prière au Moyen Age,* Senefiance 10, 449–75. Aix-en-Provence: CUERMA, 1981.

Roussel, Claude. *Conter de geste au XIVe siècle: Inspiration folklorique et écriture épique dans "La Belle Hélène de Constantinople."* Geneva: Droz, 1998.

Rychner, Jean. *La chanson de geste: Essai sur l'art épique des jongleurs.* Société de publications romanes et françaises 53. Geneva: Droz; Lille: Giard, 1955.

Suard, François. "Le motif du déguisement dans quelques chansons du cycle de Guillaume d'Orange." *Olifant* 7 (1980): 343–58.

Sunderland, Luke. *Old French Narrative Cycles: Heroism Between Ethics and Morality.* Cambridge: D. S. Brewer, 2010.

Tyssens, Madeleine. *La Geste de Guillaume d'Orange dans les manuscrits cycliques.* Paris: Belles Lettres, 1967.

Index of Proper Names

Places, Peoples, Persons, Animals, and Swords

CL = Coronation of Louis; CN = Convoy to Nîmes; CO = Conquest of Orange
Line numbers refer to the first occurrence of the proper noun in each text. For major recurring characters and places, we provide the first two and the final entries.

Place-names are generally identified in accordance with the traditional localizations established by epic scholars.

Anseaume *CO* 1093: Possibly Enserune, west of Béziers, as identified by Nelly Andrieux-Reix; associated traditionally with Garin (q.v.) in the William Cycle

Anublé *CO* 599: Saracen king, baron of Tibaut

Apollo *CO* 1172: A Saracen "god" derived probably from one of their names for the devil; not the Roman god Apollo

Apulia *CN* 1192: Former province in southeastern Italy

Arab *CL* 2498; *CO* 714: Inhabitant of Arabia; synonymous with Saracen

Arabia *CO* 727: Region in the Middle East; Saudi Arabia, or possibly any Arabic-speaking land in the Middle East or North Africa

Aragon *CO* 200, 229 . . . 1841: Tibaut's son and a Saracen king

Aragon *CL* 1780: Former kingdom, now region of Spain south of the Pyrenees, capital Zaragoza

Ardennes *CO* 184: Mountainous region today comprising parts of northeastern France, southeastern Belgium, and Luxembourg

Arrogant *CN* 518: Saracen king, baron of Tibaut

Artois *CO* 185: Former province of northwestern France, capital Arras

Atriblé *CO* 596: Saracen king, baron of Tibaut

Auberi (the Burgundian) *CN* 318: Vassal of King Louis whose fief is offered to and refused by William

Aufar (of Babylon) *CO* 972: Saracen, first king of Orange, whose helmet is given to Guielin

Auvergne *CN* 785: Province in central France, south and west of Clermont-Ferrand, including modern-day Cantal and Puy-de-Dôme

Avalon *CL* 1807: Imaginary city known for being the seat of King Arthur's court

Avars *CO* 967: Tribe from central Asia that invaded Hungary in the sixth century, associated with the Saracens in chansons de geste

Avignon *CO* 405: City in southern France on the Rhône, south of Orange and east of Nîmes

Aymer *CL* 827: William's brother

Aymeri of Narbonne *CL* 211, 574 . . . 2574; *CN* 1211, 1221 . . . 1347; *CO* 1074, 1281, 1364: William's father

Aymon *CN* 678, 707 . . . 743: Baron of King Louis, slain by William

Babylon *CO* 972: Modern-day Cairo, in Egypt, near the site of the Roman city Babylon; not the city in Mesopotamia (*see* Aufar)

Baghdad *CO* 24: Saracen land surrounding modern-day Iraq's capital Baghdad

Baillet *CN* 1276: Ox slain by Harpin

Baitaime *CO* 831: Saracen slain by William

Baratron *CL* 987: Master of Hell

Barcelona *CO* 969: City in northeastern Spain (*see* Isaac)

Barré *CN* 518: Saracen seneschal in Nîmes

Bavaria *CL* 18: Region of southeastern Germany, independent in medieval times, whose capital is now Munich

Beaucaire *CO* 227: City on the Rhône just east of Nîmes

Bedouins *CO* 1216: Saracen warriors from a nomadic North African tribe

Beelzebub *CL* 988: Demonic figure, denizen of Hell

Begue *CN* 1127: Fictitious son of the fictitious merchant Tiacre (q.v.); one of William's nephews in disguise

Berangier *CL* 569: One of Charlemagne's Twelve Peers

Berengier *CN* 330: Vassal of King Louis whose fief is offered to and refused by William

Berengier (young) *CN* 366: Son of Berengier whose fief was offered to William

Bernard (of Brabant) *CL* 212, 823; *CN* 596, 612 . . . 1130; *CO* 1092, 1329 . . . 1575: William's brother, father of Bertrand and Guielin

Berruiers *CL* 1161: Frenchmen from Berry

Berry *CN* 785: Region of central France between the Loire and the Massif Central, centered on Bourges

Bertrand *CL* 115, 275 . . . 2644; *CN* 31, 33 . . . 1297; *CO* 10, 54 . . . 1880: William's nephew, son of Bernard of Brabant

Bethlehem *CL* 727; *CO* 500: City of the Middle East where Jesus was born

Beuve (of Commarchis) *CL* 825; *CO* 1094: William's brother

Bile *CO* 346: Saracen land (*see* Goliath)

Blois *CO* 330: Royal city on the Loire in north-central France

Bonivent *CO* 1109: Saracen city (*see* Pharaoh)

Bordeaux *CL* 2000: City on the Gironde in the Aquitaine region of southwestern France

Bourreau *CO* 601, 1683: Saracen king, Aragon's uncle

Brabant *CL* 212; *CN* 596; *CO* 1365: In the Middle Ages, a region north of France, including much of modern-day Belgium and the Netherlands (*see* Bernard)

Brie *CL* 1433: Region immediately east of Paris between the Seine and Marne Rivers

Brioude *CN* 824; *CO* 8: City on the Allier in the department of Haute-Loire, south of Clermont-Ferrand; important pilgrimage site on the Regordane route

Brittany *CL* 19: Region of northwestern France that protrudes as a peninsula into the Atlantic; capital Rennes

Burgundians *CN* 205: People from Burgundy; Christian warriors

Burgundy *CN* 785; *CO* 186: Kingdom in southeastern France

Cain *CL* 625: Abel's brother and murderer, from whose lineage medieval Christians thought Muslims were descended

Calabria *CN* 1192: Region at the southernmost tip of Italy

Calvary *CL* 765: Hill on which Jesus was crucified

Canterbury *CN* 1123: Cathedral and pilgrimage city in southeastern England

Capua *CL* 305: Roman city on the Volturno near Naples in Italy, destroyed twice by Saracens in the early Middle Ages

Carthage *CL* 474: Cartagena, a city in the province of Murcia in southeastern Spain (*see* Dagobert)

Champion *CL* 1302: Saracen, Galafre's nephew

Charles / Charlemagne *CL* 15, 54 . . . 2495; *CN* 154, 163; *CO* 1364: King of the Franks, Holy Roman emperor

Chartres *CL* 2355; *CN* 529; *CO* 330: Cathedral city in central France, southwest of Paris

Cirtaige *CL* 286: William's host in Rome

Clareau (of Orange) *CN* 516; *CO* 596: Saracen baron of Tibaut, brother of Aceré

Clermont and Montferrand *CN* 833: Region in central France, around the modern-day city of Clermont-Ferrand

Clinevent *CL* 2593: Guy the German's horse, captured by William

Codroé *CO* 598: Saracen king, baron of Tibaut

Commarchis *CL* 825; *CO* 1094: Unidentified duchy ruled by Beuve (q.v.)

Cordovan *CO* 77: Made of leather from Córdoba in southern Spain

Corsolt *CL* 304, 312 . . . 2599; *CN* 11; *CO* 595: Saracen giant killed by William

Corsolt (of Mables) *CO* 595: Saracen baron of Tibaut, brother of Aceré

Cotentin *CL* 2030: Peninsula in Normandy

Cremus *CL* 304: Saracen king

Dagobert *CN* 159: Saracen king defeated by William

Dagobert (of Carthage) *CL* 2006: Saracen defeated by William

Daniel *CL* 1018; *CO* 808: Old Testament prophet saved by God from a lion's den

Denis (St.) *CL* 550, 1253 . . . 2590; *CN* 740, 1308: Legendary Christian martyr of the third century and patron of France, whose cult is centered at Saint-Denis, just north of Paris

Desramé *CN* 517; *CO* 346, 594 . . . 1716: Saracen king and ally of Tibaut

Egypt *CO* 598: Land along the Nile in North Africa

England *CN* 1122: Island nation of western Europe

Esclamors *CO* 1216: Saracen warriors

Esclavonia *CO* 627, 1277, 1304: Saracen land, meaning roughly "Land of the Saracens" in medieval French

Esquanor *CO* 1517: Saracen advisor to Aragon

Estot (of Langres) *CL* 571: One of Charlemagne's Twelve Peers

Eubron *CO* 1683: Saracen king

Eve *CL* 702: First woman

Falaise (by the Sea) *CN* 1017, 1295: In spite of its name, an inland city in Normandy (*see* Gilbert)

Fierebrace CL 251, 257 . . . 2390; CN 1049, 1103, 1338; CO 700, 722 . . . 1562: Epithet for William meaning "strong-armed"

Fleming CO 1430: Person from Flanders (*see* Gilbert)

Flemish CN 215: From the region of Flanders, between France and Frisia; Christian warriors

Floire (of Plessis) CL 1651: Knight in William's army

Foucher (of Meliant) CO 1837: French knight killed by Aragon

Foucon CN 309: Vassal of King Louis whose fief is offered to and refused by William

France CL 14, 16 . . . 2667; CN 101, 185 . . . 1482; CO 53, 55 . . . 1429: Country in western Europe, which in the Middle Ages meant the area of modern-day France mostly north and east of the Loire

Franks CL 120, 1517 . . . 2438; CN 497: Equivalent to Frenchmen throughout the poems

French, Frenchmen, Frenchwomen CL 162, 621 . . . 2635; CN 166, 205 . . . 1477; CO 75, 88 . . . 1838: People of France; Christian warriors

Frisians CN 215: A Germanic people from the Low Countries, north of Flanders; Christian warriors

Gabriel (St.) CL 400: Archangel

Gaifier (of Spoleto) CL 306, 334 . . . 2301; CN 98: King of Capua, imprisoned by Saracens

Gaifier CL 571: One of Charlemagne's Twelve Peers

Gaifier CO 1008: Saracen slain by Gilbert

Gaimar CO 1876: Bishop of Nîmes

Galafre CL 303, 351 . . . 2214: Saracen king defeated by William

Galicia CN 1195; CO 352: Province of Spain forming the northwestern corner, containing the famous medieval pilgrimage site of Santiago de Compostela

Gardon CN 1032: Small river in southern France that flows into the Gard, which itself flows into the Rhône just north of Beaucaire

Garin (of Anseaume) CL 824; CO 1093: William's brother

Garnier CN 918: Vavasor who suggests to William the ruse used to enter Nîmes

Gauldin the Brown CL 1474: William's nephew

Gautier (the Toulousain; of Toulouse) CL 1153, 1218 . . . 2597; CN 697, 713 . . . 748: William's nephew, as identified at CL 1640–41

Gautier CL 1667: Cleric at St. Martin's church in Tours; later identified as an abbot, at CL 1962

Gautier CL 572: One of Charlemagne's Twelve Peers

Gautier of Termes CN 869, 1018, 1296: Knight in William's army and leader of a vanguard

Gautier of Tudela CL 1601: Knight in William's army

Geneva CO 189: Lake on which are located the cities of Geneva and Lausanne in modern-day Switzerland

Germany CL 18; CN 1193; CO 186: In the Middle Ages, large area east of the Rhine

Giboez CO 1681: Saracen king

Gilbert (of Falaise) CN 1017: Knight in William's army

Gilbert (of Lenu, the Fleming) CO 111, 141 . . . 1881: Prisoner who escaped from Saracen city of Orange

Gilemer the Scot CN 869: Knight in William's army, and leader of a vanguard

Giles (St.) CN 577: Hermit whose cult was centered at Saint-Gilles (q.v.)

Gloriette CO 357, 517 . . . 1878: Tower in Orange where Orable resides

Goliath (of Bile) CN 517; CO 346, 594 . . . 1716: Saracen ally of Tibaut

Gondrez CN 519; CO 1684: Saracen, brother of Quinzepaumes

Gontier (of Rome) CL 1602: Knight in William's army

Griffon (of Almeria) CO 271: Saracen who built the palace in Orange

Guibert (of Andernas) CL 826: William's brother

Guibourc CN 8; CO 1872: Name given to Orable at baptism

Guielin CL 275, 407 . . . 2597; CN 595, 598 . . . 1129; CO 83, 382 . . . 1881: William's nephew, son of Bernard of Brabant

Guion CN 211: Name attributed to William's host in CL

Guy CO 184: Gilbert of Lenu's father

Guy (the German, of Germany) *CL* 2217, 2265 . . . 2581; *CN* 203: Pagan who has captured Rome; slain by William

Harpin *CN* 1080, 1114 . . . 1388; *CO* 484, 575, 699: Saracen king of Nîmes, brother of Otrant; slain by William

Haton *CL* 569: One of Charlemagne's Twelve Peers

Haucebier *CO* 1481: Saracen king

Haucebier *CO* 996: Saracen slain by William

Hermenjart *CL* 822: William's mother

Hermensant (of Tori) *CN* 319: Wife of Auberi the Burgundian

Hernaut (of Orléans) *CL* 99; *CN* 170: French baron and would-be usurper of Louis's crown; slain by William

Herod *CL* 736: Herod Antipas, known in the New Testament as King Herod

Hilary (St.) *CO* 1188: Probably St. Hilary of Poitiers (d. ca. 367), an ardent foe of Arianism, but also possibly St. Hilary of Arles (d. 449), given the geographic setting of the poem, or even the hermit St. Hilarion (d. ca. 371)

Holy Innocents *CL* 738: In Matthew 2:16, male children under the age of two slaughtered by King Herod after the Wise Men failed to return to tell him of the birth of Jesus

Hungarians *CO* 967: Members of a pagan tribe from central Europe associated with the Avars and other nomadic tribes that invaded western Europe in the early Middle Ages

Hungary *CN* 1194: Country in central Europe

Hungier *CL* 1866: Bourgeois in Tours

Isaac (of Barcelona) *CO* 969: Saracen maker of byrnie given to Guielin

James (St.) *CN* 1343; *CO* 1381: Apostle whose remains are venerated at Santiago de Compostela in northwestern Spain

Jerusalem *CL* 747: City in the Middle East where Jesus was crucified

Jesus *CL* 85, 1202, 2013; *CN* 674, 694 . . . 1091; *CO* 162, 1434 . . . 1777: Jesus of Nazareth, Son of the God of the Christians

Jews *CL* 761: Ethnic and religious group often vilified in medieval chansons de geste

Jonah *CL* 1016; *CO* 807: Old Testament prophet saved by God from the belly of a whale

Jordan *CO* 192: River in the Middle East, dividing modern-day Jordan and Israel

Joseph (of Arimathea) *CL* 779: Follower of Jesus who helped Nicodemus take Jesus down from the cross and lay him in a tomb

Joyous *CL* 1049, 2477 . . . 2580: William's sword (*see CL* 1049n)

Judas *CL* 758: Apostle who betrayed Jesus

Julien *CL* 2015: Lord of Saint-Gilles, defeated by William

Julius Caesar *CL* 468: Roman commander; builder of Rome

Krak (des Chevaliers) *CN* 1200: Crusader castle in Syria; one of the earliest and best surviving examples of a castle with rounded fortifications in stone rather than wood

Langres *CL* 571: City in the Haute-Marne department in east-central France, north of Dijon (*see* Estot)

Laon *CL* 2659; *CN* 206; *CO* 539: Cathedral and royal city northeast of Paris

Lausanne *CO* 187: City in modern-day Switzerland on the north shore of Lake Geneva

Laval-sur-Cler *CN* 890: Unidentified city in southern France

Lavardi *CN* 1056: Unidentified site of the quarry that supplied the stones for building Nîmes

Lazarus *CO* 541: Biblical figure who was raised from the dead by Jesus

Lenu *CO* 111: Birthplace of Gilbert (q.v.), in northern France or Flanders, and possibly a deformation for the rhyme of Leün (Laon?)

Le Puy, Our Lady of *CN* 825: Pilgrimage church in southern France (Haute-Loire), northeast of Orange

Lombardy *CL* 20; *CN* 1191: Region in northern Italy

Longinus *CL* 772; *CO* 504: Legendary Roman soldier who pierced Jesus's side at the Crucifixion

Lorrez *CO* 1683: Saracen king

Lot (St.) *CL* 957: Early bishop of Coutances in Normandy, Laud (also written Lois and Laudiens), for whom the modern-day city of Saint-Lô was named; chosen here for the rhyme where other manuscripts use St. Pol (Paul) and St. Job

Lotharingians *CN* 215: People from Lotharingia, the central part of the ancient Germanic kingdom extending from the North Sea to the Alps east of the Meuse and Saône rivers and west of the Rhine; Christian warriors

Louis *CL* 7, 48 . . . 2669; *CN* 48, 62 . . . 1484; *CO* 198, 1091 . . . 1574: Charlemagne's son and heir to the throne

Lovel *CN* 1277: Ox slain by Harpin

Lyon *CO* 190: City on the Rhône in south-central France

Lyons-la-Forêt *CL* 2064: Town in the modern department of Eure in Normandy; not the city of Lyon on the Rhône

Mables *CO* 595: Unidentified Saracen land (*see* Corsolt)

Mâcon *CL* 1776: Crossroads city on the Saône north of Lyon

Maudoine (of Valronne) *CO* 983: Saracen whose spear is given to Guielin

Malcuidant *CO* 638: Saracen inhabitant of Gloriette

Manessier *CL* 570: One of Charlemagne's Twelve Peers

Maretant *CO* 997 Saracen gatekeeper slain by Gilbert

Martin (St.) *CL* 1442: Bishop of Tours in France in the fourth century, buried there in the Basilica of St. Martin

Mary *CL* 171, 781 . . . 2540; *CN* 1086, 1443, 1486; *CO* 2, 29, 282: The Virgin Mary, mother of Jesus

Mary Magdalene *CL* 753; *CO* 809: One of Jesus's followers, who washed his feet

Mary Magdalene (Church of St.) *CN* 169: Church in Aix-la-Chapelle where William killed Hernaut of Orléans

Maudoine (of Nubia) *CO* 1260: Saracen boat-owner

Maurice (St.) *CO* 321: Martyr and bishop of Lyon (d. ca. 302); according to a largely discredited legend, a member of the Theban Legion sent into Gaul by the Roman emperor Maximian (r. 286–305)

Mecca *CL* 851: Pilgrimage city in modern-day Saudi Arabia sacred to Muslims

Meliant *CO* 1837: Unidentified French city or region (*see* Foucher)

Methuselah *CL* 760: Long-lived Old Testament patriarch, grandfather of Noah

Michaelmas *CN* 548: Feast of St. Michael the Archangel, celebrated on September 29

Mohammed *CL* 625, 674 . . . 1309; *CN* 890, 893 . . . 1450; *CO* 477, 492 . . . 1874: The prophet, founder of Islam

Moncontour *CO* 1123: Unidentified city

Monjoie *CL* 1921, 2307, 2590; *CN* 1399, 1420; *CO* 824, 839, 1816: Battle cry of French warriors in the Old French chansons de geste

Montbardon *CN* 216: City in northern Italy, modern-day Monbaldone

Montferrand *CN* 833: *See* Clermont

Montpellier *CL* 1147; *CN* 549: City of southern France near the Mediterranean

Montreuil (by the Sea) *CL* 2631: Montreuil-sur-mer, city in northwestern France near Calais

Mont-Saint-Michel *CL* 2028; *CN* 192: Rocky island between Brittany and Normandy with a famous abbey

Morant *CN* 518; *CO* 599: Saracen king, baron of Tibaut

Moses *CL* 1020: Old Testament prophet

Murgalé *CN* 520: Saracen king

Narbonne *CL* 211; *CN* 1211; *CO* 1074: City of southern France near the Mediterranean, southwest of Montpellier; William's city of origin (*see* Aymeri)

Navarre *CL* 20: Former kingdom, now province of northern Spain, capital Pamplona

Necene *CN* 1055: City on William's road to Nîmes, perhaps Nozières in the Gard department

Nero *CL* 988: Infamous Roman emperor, denizen of hell (*see also* Nero's Meadow)

Nero's Meadow *CL* 1014, 1778, 2467; *CN* 217, 279 . . . 1365; *CO* 810, 848, 1034: Site of St. Peter's crucifixion in Rome, and garden where Nero had Christians burned (*see CL* 1014n)

Nicodemus *CL* 779: Biblical figure who assisted in Jesus's burial

Nîmes *CN* 6, 452 . . . 1483; *CO* 13, 126 . . . 1866: Former Roman commercial center in southern France, west of Avignon, which still preserves numerous Roman monuments

Noah *CL* 718: Old Testament prophet who built an ark and survived the Flood

Norman *CL* 198; *CN* 194: Inhabitant of Normandy

Normandy *CL* 19; *CN* 1197: Ancient duchy in northwestern France (*see* Richard)

Nubia *CO* 1260: Saracen land, possibly the desert region of southern Egypt and Sudan (*see* Maudoine)

Olivier *CL* 568: Companion of Roland, one of Charlemagne's Twelve Peers

Omer (St.) *CO* 262: Follower of St. Columban and a monk at Luxeuil (Haute-Saône) for over twenty years, then bishop of Thérouanne in the Pas-de-Calais (d. ca. 670)

Orable *CL* 1417; *CN* 522; *CO* 25, 34 . . . 1867: Saracen queen, wife of King Tibaut of Africa; converts to Christianity, takes the name Guibourc, marries William (*see CL* 1417n)

Orange *CN* 7, 453 . . . 516; *CO* 17, 20 . . . 1887: Former Roman commercial center in southern France just north of Avignon, which still preserves many Roman monuments

Orient *CL* 2429; *CO* 203: Area to the east of Europe, fabled for its wealth, corresponding to modern-day definitions of the Orient

Oriflor *CO* 227: Region near Beaucaire

Orléans *CL* 99; *CN* 529: City south of Paris on the Loire; an intellectual capital in the Middle Ages (*see* Hernaut)

Orquanois *CO* 1140: Saracen advisor to Aragon

Oton *CN* 213: Saracen king slain by William

Otrant *CN* 496, 520 . . . 1461; *CO* 46, 483, 1661: Saracen king of Nîmes, brother of Harpin; defenestrated by William's men

Paris *CL* 1652, 2355 . . . 2652; *CN* 28, 199, 784; *CO* 331, 497, 1696: Most important political, intellectual, and commercial city in France in the Middle Ages

Paul (St.) *CL* 1015; *CO* 811: Apostle to the Gentiles, known from his epistles and the Acts of the Apostles (b. Tarsus ca. 5–15 AD, d. Rome ca. 62–64)

Persia *CO* 35, 340 . . . 708: Empire in the Middle East that once included modern-day Turkey, Syria, Iraq, Iran, Afghanistan, and much of Pakistan and Turkmenistan

Persians *CN* 632; *CO* 97, 229 . . . 1807: People of Persian origin, generally associated with the Saracens

Peter (Church of St.) *CN* 204: Church of the Vatican in Rome, seat of the papacy; medieval cathedral, constructed upon the grounds of Nero's Meadow (q.v.), replaced today by a much larger Renaissance structure

Peter (St.) *CL* 234; *CN* 1350; *CO* 810: Apostle

Petit Pont *CN* 28: Bridge in Paris linking the Left Bank of the Seine with the Île de la Cité, an important religious and political center throughout the Middle Ages

Pharaoh *CO* 1109, 1119 . . . 1610: Saracen king of Bonivent

Pierrelate, Pierrelarge *CL* 2005; *CN* 158: Ford and site of a battle won by William, probably Pierrelatte in the Drôme department, just north of Orange on the Rhône

Pincernie *CO* 23: Unidentified Saracen city or land

Plessis *CL* 1651: Possibly Plessis-lez-Tours (*see* Floire)

Poitiers *CL* 1644: City in east-central France, capital of the Poitou region and one of the most important cities of Roman Gaul

Poitou *CL* 1991; *CN* 1197; *CO* 325: Region north of Aquitaine along the Atlantic coast of France

Portpaillart (by the Sea) *CN* 451: Spanish city, probably in Catalonia

Quarré *CO* 835: Saracen slain by Gilbert of Lenu

Quinzepaumes *CN* 519; *CO* 597: Saracen baron of Tibaut, brother of Gondrez

Red Sea *CL* 312: Sea separating Egypt from Saudi Arabia

Regordane *CN* 840: Mountainous region of central France, crossed by a Roman road that became an important medieval trading and pilgrimage route (*see CO* 10n)

Reims *CO* 539: Royal city of eastern France, in the Champagne region

Rhône *CN* 505; *CO* 108: River of east-central and southern France, joined by the Saône at Lyon

Richard (of Rouen, of Normandy) *CL* 1384, 1423 . . . 2194; *CN* 193: Father of Acelin; defeated by William

Riquier (St.) *CO* 382: Follower of St. Columban and founder, ca. 625, of the monastery of St. Riquier (Somme), an important center of learning in the medieval period

Riviers, Val de *CN* 341: Province in the Low Countries

Robert *CN* 324: Son of Auberi the Burgundian

Roland *CL* 568: Legendary nephew of Charlemagne and one of the Twelve Peers

Romania *CN* 1193: Country in central Europe

Romans *CL* 379, 938 . . . 2305; *CN* 229: Inhabitants of Rome

Rome *CL* 42, 73 . . . 2624; *CN* 11, 135 . . . 434; *CO* 386, 963, 1628: Capital of Italy; a major pilgrimage destination in the Middle Ages

Romulus *CL* 468: Legendary founder of Rome along with his twin Remus

Rosiane *CO* 664: Orable's attendant; niece of Rubiant

Rouen *CL* 2032: Ancient Roman provincial city on the Seine west of Paris, capital of Normandy (*see* Richard)

Royaumont (by the Sea) *CO* 1682: Unidentified Saracen city on the water

Rubiant *CO* 664: Uncle of Rosiane

Russia *CL* 292: Region of northeastern Europe, corresponding to modern-day Russia

Saint Bernard Pass *CL* 273, 282 . . . 2253; *CN* 216: At the border between Switzerland and Italy, the main pass on the route between France and Italy throughout the Middle Ages

Saint-Denis *CL* 1445, 2495: City north of Paris whose early Gothic church holds the tomb of St. Denis, patron of Paris (q.v.)

Saint-Gilles *CL* 2011; *CN* 549, 876, 891; *CO* 7: Pilgrimage city on the Regordane route, near Nîmes

Salatré *CO* 746 Saracen captured by William in Nîmes; escaped to Orange

Saracens *CL* 9, 302 . . . 1314; *CN* 138, 349 . . . 1426; *CO* 63, 97 . . . 1828: In medieval times, any person of whatever origin (Turkish, Arabic, North African, etc.) thought to be Muslim; generalized name for any non-Christian people

Savaris *CL* 1475: William's nephew

Scotland *CN* 1198: Region of northern Britain

Sens *CO* 497: Cathedral city in central France southeast of Paris

Sicily *CN* 1192: Island off the southern tip of Italy, an important kingdom throughout the Middle Ages

Simon Magus *CL* 1019: Simon the Magician, who attempted to purchase spiritual powers from the Apostles Peter and John, thus giving his name to the term "simony"

Simon the Leper *CL* 751: Jesus's host

Slavs *CL* 830; *CN* 349, 853 . . . 1288; *CO* 63, 145 . . . 1679: People of eastern European origin; like Saracen and Turk, a generalized name for any non-Christian people, usually Muslim

Sorant *CN* 1127: Fictitious son of the fictitious merchant Tiacre (q.v.); one of William's nephews in disguise

Sorbant (of Venice) *CO* 624: Young Saracen man

Sorgalé *CO* 597: Saracen king, baron of Tibaut

Sorgremont (by the Sea) *CO* 600: Saracen city

Sorgue *CO* 404: Tributary of the Rhône just north of Avignon

Spain *CL* 2239; *CN* 450, 481 . . . 1196; *CO* 6, 201 . . . 1685: Country in western Europe that included parts of modern-day southern France in the Middle Ages

Spoleto *CL* 334; *CN* 97: Capital of an ancient duchy in modern-day Umbria in central Italy

Stephen (St.) *CO* 1418: Of several possible St. Stephens, most likely the first martyr of the Christian church, slain in Jerusalem ca. 35 AD

Susce *CO* 23: Unidentified Saracen city or land

Synagon *CO* 484: Saracen king of Nîmes

Syrian *CO* 1748: From Syria

Tabarie *CO* 24: Saracen city, perhaps Tiberias on the Sea of Galilee in present-day Israel

Tenebrez *CL* 303: Saracen king

Termes *CN* 869, 1018, 1296: City held by Gautier of Termes in epics of the William Cycle; possibly Ax-les-Termes in the Ariège valley southeast of Foix

Tervagant *CN* 1098; *CO* 477: Saracen god

Tiacre *CN* 1136: Alias adopted by William in his merchant's disguise

Tibaut (of Africant) *CN* 9; *CO* 27, 35 . . . 1715: Orable's husband; also called Tibaut of Persia, Tibaut of Spain, Tibaut of Esclavonia, Tibaut the Slav, Tibaut of Aragon, Tibaut the Arab

Tiber *CL* 1300; *CN* 209: River of central Italy that flows through Rome

Tori *CN* 319: Possibly Turin, Italy (*see* Hermensant)

Tornemont (of Valsone) *CO* 976: Saracen whose sword is given to Guielin

Tortolouse *CN* 451: Spanish city, perhaps Tortosa on the Ebro in Catalonia

Toulouse *CL* 1218: City in southwestern France on the Garonne (*see* Gautier)

Toulousain *CN* 697: From Toulouse (*see* Gautier)

Tours *CL* 1442: Pilgrimage site on the Loire south of Paris, associated with St. Martin (q.v.)

Tudela *CL* 1601: Possibly Tudela in the Spanish province of Navarre (*see* Gautier)

Turfier *CO* 998: Saracen slain by Guielin

Turks *CL* 550, 810 . . . 1128; *CN* 268, 349; *CO* 113, 196 . . . 1644: People of Turkish origin; like Saracen and Slav, a generalized name for any non-Christian people, usually Muslim

Tuscany *CL* 20; *CN* 1194: Region of west central Italy, capital Florence

Twelve Peers *CL* 573: Charlemagne's most distinguished barons, including Roland; according to the *Song of Roland,* all were slain at the Battle of Roncevaux. The number twelve has symbolic value (e.g., the Twelve Apostles) rather than historical accuracy.

Valdon *CO* 1246: Unidentified Saracen city in North Africa, possibly the same as Vaudon, Valdonne, Valronne. In the William epics, as well as in other chansons de geste such as the *Song of Roland,* Saracen cities often begin with Val- or Vau- meaning "valley" or "pit."

Valdonne *CO* 977: Unidentified Saracen city

Valronne *CO* 983: Unidentified Saracen city (*see* Maudoine)

Valsone *CO* 976: Unidentified Saracen city (*see* Tornemont)

Valsore *CN* 501: Unidentified Saracen city near Nîmes

Valsure *CN* 501: Unidentified Saracen city near Nîmes, possibly the same as Vaseüre, Valsore, and Valsone

Vaseüre *CN* 494: Saracen city near Nîmes held by Otrant

Vaudon *CO* 525: Unidentified Saracen city in North Africa, probably the same as Valdon

Vauquois *CO* 1134: Unidentified mountain pass

Venice *CN* 1202; *CO* 624: City in northern Italy on the Adriatic Sea (*see* Sorbant)

Vermandois *CO* 185: Plateau region north of Paris, an independent county until 1191

Virgin *CL* 723, 1084, 2540; *CN* 272; *CO* 500, 542 . . . 806: The Virgin Mary, mother of Jesus

Voirecombe *CO* 978: Unidentified Saracen city

Wales *CN* 1199: Region in eastern Britain, corresponding to modern-day Wales

William *CL* 8, 113 . . . 2670; *CN* 5, 17 . . . 1483; *CO* 9, 14 . . . 1886: William of Orange, legendary epic hero, also called Short-Nosed William, Fierebrace

Yvoire *CL* 569: One of Charlemagne's Twelve Peers

Yvon *CL* 569: One of Charlemagne's Twelve Peers

CATHERINE M. JONES is the Josiah Meigs Distinguished Teaching Professor of French and Provençal at the University of Georgia. She specializes in the Old French epic and is the author of *An Introduction to the Chansons de Geste*.

WILLIAM W. KIBLER is the author of *An Introduction to Old French* and the translator and/or editor of many Old French texts, including *Huon de Bordeaux*, the romances of Chrétien de Troyes, and most recently *Gui de Bourgogne*.

LOGAN E. WHALEN is professor of French at the University of Oklahoma. His research focuses on twelfth- and thirteenth-century Old French narrative texts, especially on the works of Marie de France.